Waterford Whispers News is a national phenomenon. With over 500,000 fans on Facebook and three million page views on the website every month, it is Ireland's leading satirical news site, providing an addictive mix of relevant, topical and brilliantly funny stories. WWN is run from Tramore in County Waterford by son-of-two Colm Williamson.

For all the latest news, visit
www.waterfordwhispersnews.com

And follow WWN on Facebook at
www.facebook.com/WhispersNews

PRAISE FOR WATERFORD WHISPERS NEWS

'Waterford Whispers News has been my daily
go-to for unbiased, fact-based news.'
DAVE McELFATRICK (CYANIDE & HAPPINESS)

'WWN has reminded a lot of Irish people what biting satire is.'
EPIC NEWS WITH PETER & CHRIS

'Gas bastards'
THE RUBBERBANDITS

'I laughed until I cried and then I ate some cheese.'
CHRIS O'DOWD

ww news

Waterford Whispers News

YOU COULDN'T MAKE IT UP!

·THE·
BLACK
·STAFF·
PRESS

Waterford Whispers News is a satirical newspaper and comedy website published by
Waterford Whispers News. Waterford Whispers News uses invented names in all
the stories in this book, except in cases when public figures are being satirised.
Any other use of real names is accidental and coincidental.

First published in 2016 by
Blackstaff Press
4D Weavers Court
Linfield Road
Belfast
BT12 5GH

Designed by seagulls.net
Printed in Northern Ireland by W&G Baird

ISBN 978-0-85640-988-2

www.blackstaffpress.com
www.waterfordwhispersnews.com

CONTENTS

I would like to thank my co-writers Karl Moylan and Gerry McBride for all their hard work, and also our cartoonist Rory Thompson for his beautiful artwork and book cover. Thanks to Alan McCabe on drums. Ally Grace on bass. And a big massive huge thank you to our readers for sharing our content online and making us laugh uncontrollably with yer brilliant comments. Love, peace and respect y'all.

A word from our owner, trillionaire Declan O'Ryan

We are proud to introduce our owner – business tycoon, trillionaire, and champion of the people Declan O'Ryan. Mr O'Ryan, who was born in Waterford and now runs some of the biggest newspaper publishers in the country, including WWN, along with several thousand radio stations, petrol stations, power stations, Garda stations, train stations as well as counties Leitrim, Roscommon and the Isle Of Man, has kindly taken the time to speak to you, our readers, directly and give you some insight into the exciting world of business and finance.

Welcome, Irish peasants. If you're reading this now, it means you are interested in me and also able to read, so well done on that front. You're a credit to your parents and the Catholic school system that reared you.

Last week, as I sat here in my Isle Of Man residence, I received an email from your Taoiseach Aiden Kenny, or whatever his name is, requesting me to 'open up' a bit more to those of you at home, as it appears many people

don't seem to understand me or my business practices, leaving many rumours and false truths circulating about me, which I will not mention here as I would probably have to sue myself for doing so.

Let me tell you a bit about myself. I come from a humble background. My dad was a poor investment banker, so growing up was tough on me as we had to scrape by on whatever the head chef served us. I basically lived meal-to-meal, course-to-course, growing up in one of the toughest neighbourhoods in County Waterford, Lismore.

I first realised I had a nose for business on my fifteenth birthday, when my dad's politician friend gave me a birthday card containing several site deeds with planning permission for housing estates. I was absolutely thrilled that my dad wanted to put them all in my name. He even gave me my own bank account with several million in it. It was the first time that he really talked to me and I'll never forget his words – 'The money's mine, it just happens to be in your bank account.' It was one of the few conversations we had.

Nothing is handed to you in life, you have to earn it: stern words, but I hate hearing people who had nothing, like me, moan about it.

By the time I left school, I was already a multi-billionaire and had an impressive property portfolio. But truth be told, I wasn't happy. I wanted more. I heard how people talked about my father and his sound political friends. It seemed everyone was out to get him at the time, because they were jealous of his success. But that's Ireland for you: full of begrudgers just waiting to pounce on whatever financial scandal you're involved in.

In 1998, I decided enough was enough, and that I was going to change everyone's opinion by buying the source of all their opinions – the national press. Besides, chicks love men in power and I was only gagging to lose my virginity at the age of thirty-five. The thing is, in Ireland, you gotta buy the media first. When you own the media, you get the power. When you get the power, then you get the women.

Finally, in 2003, on my fortieth birthday, I found the woman of my dreams, Ching Hu, on a Thai bride dating site, and I have never looked back since. She accepted me, my bank account and my inverted penis. She didn't once laugh at me naked, as other women had done.

Today, I own 98 per cent of Ireland's media outlets, including this fine publication you're reading right now. I am delighted to finally get my voice heard and over the coming weeks, I'll be clearing my family's good name.

Until next time, Slane my care ah.

D

Rock legend Animal dies, aged 66

Tributes have been flooding in from across the world following the death of Animal, the legendary drummer with rock outfit Dr Teeth and The Electric Mayhem.

Fans of the supergroup were shocked to learn of the passing of the iconic percussionist, who passed away at just 66 following a short

illness. Remaining band members Dr Teeth, Janice, Zoot and Floyd Pepper took to the group's Facebook fan page to announce the sad news earlier today.

'We will never forget you, brother,' read the statement from the band. 'You kept rocking 'til the very end. Be at peace now, and we'll play again in that great Muppet theatre in the sky.'

Dr Teeth and The Electric Mayhem had been performing together for several years before their breakout performance on *The Muppet Show* in 1975. The band were invited to continue as resident artists on the show, but it was Animal's trademark intensity that won him

the hearts of fans across the world. His popularity led to appearances in every Muppet movie released, with his last role in 2014's *Muppets: Most Wanted*.

'Although he had already been diagnosed with Threadbaring Syndrome, you would have never known he was sick,' said Fozzie Bear, speaking about the filming of *M:MW*.

'I'd ask him if he was feeling all right, and he'd just say "ANIMAL!!! HAAAAH!!!!". That was ... that was just Animal, you know.'

Other Muppets were quick to add their tributes, with Miss Piggy stating that Animal was 'a driving force in her life', and the Swedish Chef adding that Animal always knew 'how tee bork de bork'.

CELEBRITY NEWS

Mark Hamill has been forced at gunpoint to trace his roots back to Ireland during the filming of *Star Wars: Episode VIII* in Donegal.

Despite him insisting that he was fairly sure that he had no Irish heritage, members of the Irish Society of Everyone Is Irish (ISEII) stated that with a name like Hamill, he 'must be Irish surely'.

In scenes reminiscent of the time Barack Obama was forced to say he was descended from people in Offaly, Hamill was kidnapped by ISEII officers as he relaxed in his trailer during a break from filming. The actor was then told that he had ten minutes to find some link to Ireland or he'd be 'sent to a grave far far away'.

Luke Skywalker traces heritage back to the Bundoran Skywalkers

Finding no genealogical link to Irish ancestors, a desperate Hamill was nevertheless released after finding a family of Skywalkers who lived in Bundoran in the 1700s, which appeased his captors enough that they agreed to let him go.

'See, another Irishman!' beamed Cathal O'Laughneassa, chief spokesperson for the ISEII. 'For a while there, it looked like Mr Hamill thought he could

visit Ireland and we wouldn't connect him to a family that was chased out of here by the Brits centuries ago. It takes us a while sometimes, but we always find a link in the end. Add Mr Hamill to our list of people that are Irish! Ireland Abu!'

Hamill was allowed to return to the set of *Star Wars*, but only after he had been photographed tearfully sipping a pint of Guinness.

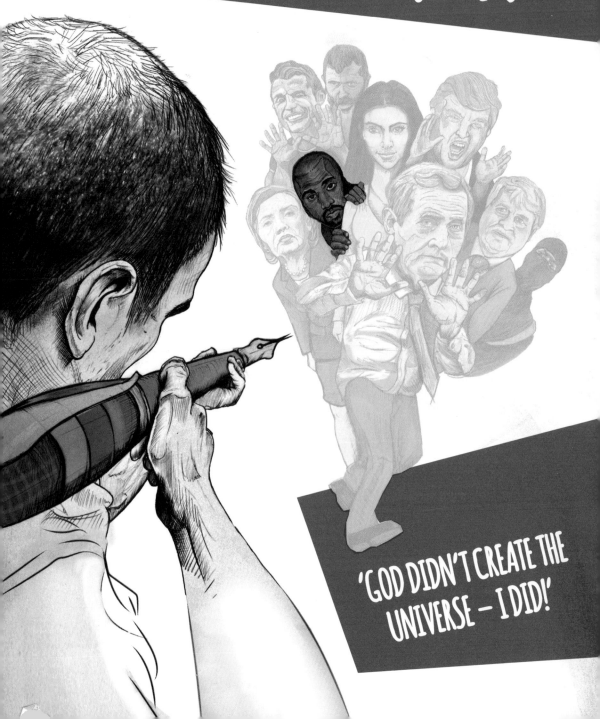

Angelina Jolie straight down the council for a house

With no other option open to her than the street, Angelina Jolie has applied for assistance in finding accommodation for her and her children from her local council following her unexpected separation from husband Brad Pitt.

Although Jolie is a successful actor, director and humanitarian, the soaring cost of housing combined with childcare costs for her six kids has left her with no other choice than to leave work after splitting with Pitt for reasons as yet unknown.

Jolie and her children have been placed in emergency accommodation in a hotel by her local council while her application is processed, and she has not been given any indication as to how long that will take. The 41-year-old

is said to be heartbroken at having to quit work, but felt she had no other choice than to do what was best for her family in these trying times.

Meanwhile, gossip sources with perfect family circumstances have criticised Jolie for what they see as her greed, with many asking why they should have to pay for her to be housed.

'Six kids from four fathers, and she's asking the taxpayer to pay the bill?' argued one local charmer.

'Who asked her to get married and have all them kids in the first place? What did she expect? She should

have considered that maybe her marriage would break up some day and she would be left with more than she could cope with. I have two kids, and I've looked into my crystal ball and can assure you that me and my wife will be together forever in our house and nothing will ever change that. Why can't all families do that? Fuck the free house – a hostel is good enough for her.'

Meanwhile, free from the hassle of having to look after six kids, Brad Pitt has moved into an affordable one-bedroom flat and has therefore escaped any sort of public scrutiny.

'There is no conspiracy – I'm dead,' confirms Tupac Shakur

Legendary rapper Tupac Shakur has denied rumours that he is still alive, stating that there is no conspiracy and that he is still very much dead.

Speaking from his home in an undisclosed location in South America, Mr Shakur lashed out at conspiracy theorists who claim the 44-year-old faked his own death, and pleaded with them to stop as it was 'upsetting his remaining family'.

'This whole thing is ridiculous,' he told the *Guardian* newspaper in an exclusive interview on Monday. 'A member of Suge Knight's crew rolled up on the left side of our ride and sunk five slugs into me. I was dead as a motherfucker.'

Showing his scars, Shakur, commonly known as 2Pac, proved to the reporter that he was indeed shot in the chest, pelvis, right hand and thigh, thereby confirming the murder.

'Man, if I was still alive, I'd still be making albums and not holed up in some shack in Nicaragua, living off millions of dollars of royalties,' he explained. 'No sir, I'm absolutely dead and there's not a nigga in the world tha' can do anythin' 'bout it.'

The final confirmation of his death comes just months after it was reported that a film about his life was due to start filming.

The movie – which has the rights to use the iconic rapper's music – will cover key areas of his life, leading up to his tragic death.

'I can't wait to see it,' Shakur commented. 'The script looks great.'

Dáithí Ó Sé arrested trying to buy extra fadas on the black market

Beloved TV personality Dáithí Ó Sé has been disgraced after an undercover sting operation by a special Garda task force caught the Kerryman red-handed attempting to buy extra fadas for his name on the black market.

Fadas are highly regulated, and it is illegal to add them to your name. However, several fada smugglers operate in Gaeltacht areas, and transport large quantities of unused fadas to the nation's capital.

The modern Irish TV landscape has changed in recent years, placing greater importance on 'Irishness', which has led to many television personalities being favoured for their Irish-sounding names and looks. Ó Sé has both of these in abundance – but when the availability of extra black market fadas became widespread, the 39-year-old found himself muscled out of well-paid gigs.

'Depending on what sector you're working in, a high number of fadas can be invaluable,' explained Garda John Dunne, head of the task force that arrested Ó Sé. 'Let's say you work for Bord Fáilte or Bord na Móna, they're dealing with big businesses from the US and elsewhere that lap that shit up, so employers fast track individuals with the most Irish names, with a preference for multiple fadas.'

Ó Sé was caught trying to buy just a single fada in an alleyway adjacent to Dublin's Smithfield market from an undercover Garda. He was carrying €5,000 in cash.

'I was always teased when I was a kid by the other boys for having an "i" in my name without a fada on it,' Ó Sé confessed to arresting Gardaí. 'You need the extra fadas in this TV game. You'd want to see the amount of corporate gigs Aóíbhínn Ní Shúílléábháín got after she bought her extra fadas. It was her that turned me on to it,' Ó Sé is alleged to have said as he was placed in the back of a police van.

If convicted, Ó Sé could serve up to three years in prison.

Angela Lansbury comes out of retirement to solve Regency Hotel murder mystery

Veteran British actress and honorary Irish citizen Angela Lansbury has been approached by An Garda Síochána and has agreed to use the skills she learned on *Murder, She Wrote* to help solve the recent spate of murders in Dublin.

Lansbury, 90, was in Dublin to collect a lifetime achievement award at the Bord Gáis Energy Theatre as part of the Audi Dublin International Film Festival. It is believed that she left the event and went straight to the Regency Hotel to see if she could find any clues that would help investigations into the murder of a gang member murdered at a boxing weigh-in event recently.

Bringing back the investigative powers she honed playing amateur sleuth Jessica Fletcher for nearly twenty years, Lansbury visited the scene where a second man with connections to the Dublin drug trade was gunned down, while a senior member of the Gardaí shook his head and told her she was wasting her time.

'I thought there were a lot of murders in Cabot Cove, but Dublin is getting ridiculous,' said Lansbury, taking a break from snooping around where she doesn't belong. 'But I think I'm close to cracking this case. All I need to do is organise a meeting with the senior members of each gang so I can trick them into confessing to these crimes while

the cops are listening. The bad guys get arrested, and the rest of us have a big laugh about it down at the station.

'It'll take about an hour, tops,' she added.

UPDATE: A man linked to the shooting has handed himself in to the guards, after realising it was only a matter of time before Lansbury caught him.

CELEBRITY NEWS

Irish Actress Kate Winslet Wins Golden Globe

Irish actress Kate Winslet appeared to be completely in shock when she won a Best Supporting Actress Golden Globe for her role in the *Steve Jobs* biopic.

The Irish-born celebrity described co-star and fellow Irishman Michael Fassbender as 'a legend' and 'an amazing colleague and friend'.

'I'm not just saying that because I'm Irish,' 40-year-old Winslet told WWN. 'It was an absolute honour to work with Michael on this movie as we had crossed paths numerous times in our younger days working in Ireland. I'm delighted to be bringing this award home to Ballyreading. Come on you boys in green!'

In *Jobs*, Winslet played Joanna Hoffman, a Polish immigrant who worked as an Apple marketing executive.

'I think that being an emigrant helped a lot with my role as Joanna,' the farmer's daughter explained. 'After all, the Irish and Polish basically built the bloody place!'

In other categories, British actress Saoirse Ronan failed to grab the Best Actress award after being nominated in the category for her role in *Brooklyn*.

Apple stock plummets amid fears of new U2 album

Shares in tech giant Apple took an unprecedented tumble today, as Irish rock group U2 announced their next album was nearing completion, and could possibly see a release before the end of this year.

The news sent icy blasts of pure fear through the souls of iTunes users worldwide, as they remembered the dark days and weeks that surrounded the last U2 album, which they were forced to receive in 2014.

With the release of the upcoming *Songs Of Experience* looking like it will skirt dangerously close to the release of the iPhone 7, markets across the world reacted violently amid fears that a repeat of the publicity stunt would send users screaming away from iOS in favour of an operating system that comes without any threat of Bono showing up in your record collection.

'Apple lost nearly $5bn from its worldwide value overnight,' said one flabbergasted stockbroker. 'CEO Tim Cook needs to step forward and assure people that the fourteenth U2 album will not be shoved into their iTunes like the last one was, or this sell-off is likely to continue for months. People worldwide are panicking. We've had reports coming in that some people heard about *Songs Of Experience* and immediately rushed to eBay to try and sell their iPhones. And, honestly, who could blame them?'

U2 frontman Bono was available for comment on everything, for those who wanted to listen to him.

The Year in Stats

God killed a record number of famous people this year, clocking up an impressive 90,567 RIPs.

Adele's ex given new identity, moved to safe place

A former lover of the chart-topping singer Adele has been relocated to what police are describing as 'a safe zone' after being given a new identity amid fears that his life was in danger.

The name of the man has not been released to the public in order to protect him from the multi-award-winning recording artist, who has become known for not taking a break-up lightly.

Although the pair only dated for a fortnight back in 2004, Adele has written eighteen songs about how much she hated the man and how he wrecked her life. These tracks go on to suggest that, although she is much happier now, she still holds a serious grudge and will never forgive him as long as he lives.

'The amount of time Adele has spent writing songs about this person suggests that he is in considerable danger,' said Malcolm Sutting, spokesperson for the Metropolitan Police's ex-boyfriend relocation programme.

'We are sure that he never thought it would come to this when he asked her out for a Nandos over a decade ago. Although the man is now safe, we would urge others to consider their future before asking Adele if she fancies going to the cinema or for a walk in town.'

If you have been in a relationship with Adele and feel your life is in danger, please contact your local police service.

BREAKING NEWS

Baz Ashmawy charged with fifty counts of attempted murder

Irish TV and radio personality Baz Ashmawy has been arrested during a dawn raid on his home by Gardaí, following an investigation into as many as fifty counts of attempted murder.

Ashmawy, 40, was hauled out of his home before 7 a.m. by members of Special Branch. Although no official statements have been issued, Ashmawy was heard yelling at police that they'd 'got it all wrong'.

It is believed that the fifty charges all stem from attempts on the life of one Nancy Ashmawy, who Gardaí believe is known to the suspect.

'Following up on information provided to us by Sky, we put together a profile of Mr Ashmawy which led to his arrest this morning,' said Superintendent Charles Morris during a press conference today.

'Sixteen officers armed with pepper spray and Tasers breached the front door of Ashmawy's property at 6:45 a.m, and managed to finish kicking the shit out of him by 7:15. The suspect is now in custody, after a short hearing this morning during which he was refused bail. We believe we're looking at someone who could become one of the country's leading serial murderers, and we're giving ourselves pats on the back all round for bringing him in.'

Morris went on to state that as Ashmawy's first fifty attempts on the life of Nancy Ashmawy were unsuccessful, he could possibly have been in the process of developing fifty more.

CELEB PROFILES

MICHAEL FLATLEY

AGE: 58

FACE: kind of stuck in that one expression at all times. Bad Botox, we think.

JOB: moving his legs up and down really quickly while looking straight ahead and smiling like a teenage boy who has just seen his first set of breasts.

IN THE NEWS FOR: selling his legs at auction after retiring from the Irish-dancing game. Set to fetch as much as €10 million.

MOST ICONIC MOMENT: his Riverdance performance at the Eurovision in which he levitated forty feet above the stage and performed a liver transplant on an elderly woman using only his feet.

KYLIE JENNER

AGE: 19

JOB: beats us.

NUMBER OF ORIFICES YET TO BE SEEN ON SNAPCHAT: 0

KNOWN FOR: endorsing every product known to man in an attempt to squeeze money out of young and impressionable followers as well as not-so-young followers who should know better.

WELL KNOWN FOR: looking nothing like herself.

FAMOUS FOR: being the subject of two thousand final-year arts theses which use her as a basis for their argument that humankind is beyond help, and culture as we know it has disintegrated into a steaming pile of faeces.

INFAMOUS FOR: being a vacuous symptom of all that is wrong with the world or, depending on who you talk to, a body-positive feminist icon who blazes a trail for so many young women.

NOTORIOUS FOR: causing your dad to repeatedly ask you to explain just who she is and what she does.

PHOTOS TAKEN IN THE LAST MINUTE: 4,567

---

f Inspirational Quote of the Year

'It takes more muscles to frown than it does to smile. I have done no research whatsoever to back up those claims.'

BEYONCÉ

AGE: fierce

FAMOUS FOR: being fierce

TALENTS: being fierce

MUSIC: fierce

I'M NOT A FAN TO BE HONEST: shut up, yes you are. Everyone is. She be Bey, Queen Bey. She fierce. So fan up or face the fierce consequences.

FLAWS: none. She's too fierce for that.

STRENGTHS: turning grown women into obedient subjects who do her bidding. Fierce.

FIERCE: fierce

WHAT'S NEXT FOR HER: something fierce

KANYE WEST

AGE: 39

OCCUPATION: rapper, artiste, giving the mentally ill a bad name.

HOBBIES: making his wife, Kim Kardashian, relevant.

LATEST WORK OF GENIUS: a finger painting, described by people who have no idea what they're talking about as a 'masterpiece, a work of genius'. Only a gifted man such as Kanye would think to paint something worse than a two-year-old.

TALENTS: an ability to look sad in 90 per cent of photos taken of him.

MOST LIKELY TO SAY: imma let you finish but God didn't create the universe – I did.

LEAST LIKELY TO SAY: stop paying attention to me, I'm full of shit.

ANGRY AT: having his creativity stifled at every turn by 'the system' despite being independently wealthy and one of the most recognisable people on the planet.

TAYLOR SWIFT

AGE: 26

HEIGHT: the envy of many, many women.

KNOWN FOR: empowering women. Owning, crushing, rocking and winning at various things.

OCCUPATION: singer; deflecting the media's attempt at ruining her good name.

BIGGEST HITS: 'Craic Whore Blues', 'Shake It Off', 'The US Taxation System Needs A Serious Overhaul As Part Of An Overall Effort To Redistribute Wealth Equally Across Society'

FAMOUS FRIENDS: Ed Sheeran, Ellie Goulding, Selena Gomez, the Dalai Lama, Charles Manson.

CURRENTLY DATING: the identity of her latest paramour will have changed fourteen times by the end of this sentence.

CHILDREN: are the future.

FAVOURITE THINGS: peace on earth.

DID YOU KNOW: it is illegal on the internet not to like her.

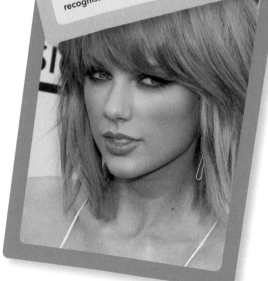

Everything you wanted to know about Daniel O'Donnell but were too afraid to ask

Always been curious about Donegal's most famous export, but didn't want to be laughed at by die-hard fans for not knowing everything about Mr O'Donnell? Well, WWN is here to fill you in and answer all your questions.

What was Daniel's childhood like?

Daniel O'Donnell of course spent his formative years in the womb, and then in Donegal, but a trip to a Gaeltacht in Miami, Florida, in the US of A made the biggest impression on Ireland's most angelic voice.

The Gaeltacht, located on Miami's Virginia Key Beach, was known for its excellent standard in teaching Irish, but was also plagued by youth gangs made up of Cuban immigrants.

It was here, during his three weeks in Miami, that Daniel was forced into a series of knife fights on the unforgiving corner spots, where the city's heroin selling was done.

Daniel maintains he learned a great deal of Irish while in Miami but regrets being forced into killing three teenagers in bloody flick-blade battles.

He's been on Strictly Come Dancing, hasn't he?

Why yes he has! Top marks for your O'Donnell knowledge, or as it is known amongst his fans O'Donnelledge.

Is he any good at dancing?

While still discovering his voice, Daniel spent a year in Paris as a teen, training in the world-famous Paris Opera Ballet under the tutelage of the celebrated ballet dancer Rudolf Nureyev. Daniel was, by all accounts, a majestic ballerina, who glided across the floor like a piece of silk caught by a most gentle gust of wind.

Nureyev feared O'Donnell would eclipse him and so, at the end of a draining dance-off one night, the Russian took a crowbar to Daniel's legs and brutally smashed them to pieces. So, to answer your question: no, he's a bit shit.

Is his music all that gay hymn shite?

Daniel has experimented with a number of styles over the years, experiencing his biggest success with an album entitled *Daniel Does Slipknot*. His 12-track cover version album of all of Slipknot's best-known songs won him new fans in the under-85s age bracket, and culminated in headline sets at the Download and Fields of Rock festivals in 2004.

Does he have a penis?

Contrary to misconceptions, Daniel O'Donnell was not the subject of the *Father Ted* episode *Night of the Nearly Dead*. In fact, Daniel himself wrote the episode about a rival singer from Donegal who went missing a year before following a sleepover at Daniel's house. He has not been found to this day. Daniel does of course have a penis but lost contact with it some time in the late '90s – sadly, they haven't spoken since.

I quite fancy him. Is he single?

Oh, hard luck, he is actually happily married to Majella O'Donnell, who for legal reasons is beyond ridicule.

I'm not very political, but does Daniel have any views?

Famously, he came out in support of gay marriage, providing the Yes side with a much-needed boost in the run-up to the referendum. He was also head of the Cambodian army during the period when the Khmer Rouge had a brutal stranglehold on the Cambodian people. So, no, he's not big into politics either.

Mortifying scenes at Oscars as all men show up wearing the same thing

There were red faces all round at the recent Academy Awards ceremony in Los Angeles, after almost every single man in attendance showed up wearing the same outfit.

From George Clooney to Sylvester Stallone, all of the male attendees arrived at the glitzy event wearing a black suit, white shirt, and a tie or dicky bow.

Heated arguments broke out as actors, directors and producers debated among themselves as to who should be allowed to keep wearing their clothes and who should be forced to go home and change, with Leonardo Di Caprio heard exclaiming that he should keep wearing his tuxedo as he 'wears it best'.

Fashion journalists and paparazzi wasted no time in tearing into the men, posting scathing criticisms on Instagram and Twitter that were lapped up by a worldwide audience of actor-shamers.

'The fucking state of some of these lads, seriously,' said one tabloid journalist in a fifteen-page spread entitled 'Actors In Red Carpet Mortification'.

'Honestly, what were they thinking. Some of them have made a little bit of effort to change the colour of their dinner jackets, but that's about it. It's like they thought they weren't going to suffer the scrutiny that their female counterparts face at every red-carpet event they attend. Absolute spanners.'

The massive fashion faux pas was compounded by rumours that some of the actors were wearing the same outfits they had worn to the Golden Globes ceremony nearly two months before.

Sources confirm Chris Brown has his poor mother's heart broken

Following yet another skirmish with the law and more allegations of violence against women, sources close to R&B star Chris Brown have confirmed that his poor mother's heart is broken, and that she 'doesn't know what to do with him at all at all'.

The singer has a history of violent behaviour, including an attack in 2009 on then-girlfriend Rihanna, which resulted in a five-year probation sentence. Brown's mother was said to be 'very disappointed' in her son at the time, stating that 'he wasn't reared like that, so he wasn't'.

More recently, Brown, 27, was involved in a tense stand-off with police in Los Angeles, amid reports that he had threatened a woman with a gun and then attempted to have her sign a non-disclosure agreement to prevent her from reporting the incident.

Police swarmed on Brown's home as friends and family pleaded with the singer to co-operate, resulting in an arrest late last night. Sources have confirmed that poor oul Joyce

'isn't the better of it yet', and hopes her son 'rights himself'.

'She's in bits, the poor crater,' confirmed one of Joyce's neighbours, as she smoked at the front gate of her house. 'He's a pure pup that child, doesn't think of his mam at all. Away gallivanting with them rap lads. And the tattoos on them – Jeeeesus. She keeps going on about how nice he was in school. Well I'll tell you, if he was my child, there'd be manners on him.'

Adding shame to injury, detectives visited Brown's mam in her house in a marked squad car, so now everyone

in the neighbourhood knows something is up.

Luke Skywalker controversially relocated to rural parish

Locals in a small Kerry community have raised questions as to why an elderly member of a religious order who was involved in a controversial incident with young people was relocated to their locality, after it was revealed that Luke Skywalker was living on an island off the coast of the Iveragh peninsula.

Skywalker, a high-ranking member of the Jedi order, was spotted on the island of Skellig Michael by passing fishermen

who recognised him from his days as the saviour of the known galaxy.

Despite his glorious past, rumours abound that Skywalker was forced to leave his position as a trainer in the Jedi academy following a hushed-up incident.

The appearance of Skywalker in Kerry is the first time in Irish history that an elderly cleric has been relocated to a remote parish under a veil of secrecy.

'We don't mind him in the parish, as long as he's not going to be causing any trouble,' said one local we interviewed. 'Somebody saw fit to tell him to come down this way until whatever trouble he was in had all blown over, and we don't question anything like that around here. Sure, if he was a danger to us in any way, we're sure the guards would have been on to him by now.'

Questions are being raised as to how Skywalker managed to get to such a high position within the Jedi order, with many suggesting his father might have got him the job.

Best-ever Irish songs,
as voted by WWN readers

1. *'Maniac 2000'* – Mark McCabe (Jedward Acid House Remix)

2. *'I'd Love a Go of Your Box'* – Daniel O'Donnell feat. B*Witched

3. The A -Team *theme tune* – written by Irishman and noted TV composer Seamus Hanratty

4. *'Born in the USA'* – Bruce Springsteen (he probably has some Irish blood in him down the line)

5. *'Can't Touch This'* – MC Hammer (written by Bono & Enya)

Calvin Harris releases new single 'Baggy Fanny'

Scottish music producer and DJ Calvin Harris surprised his fans recently by dropping a new single called 'Baggy Fanny'.

'Just something I've worked up over the last day or two,' tweeted Harris to his 7.9 million Twitter followers. 'Hope you enjoy it – it felt good to release something that is close to my heart.'

The 3.49-minute track is reminiscent of Harris's earlier work, and features just one lyric – 'Baggy fanny, never seen such a baggy fanny' – set to a pumping techno beat.

The track comes complete with two B-sides titled 'You can hear an echo' and 'Tie a board across my back', as well as a number of remixed versions of 'Baggy Fanny', including 'Baggy Fanny – Clown Pockets Mix'.

Harris, 32, recently went through a messy break-up from pop sensation Taylor Swift, which resulted in an angry Twitter spat. Although Swift is known for basing her songs on previous relationships, Harris assures fans that his new track isn't based on anyone in particular.

'Baggy Fanny' is the first single from Harris's upcoming album, 'Throwing a White Pudding into the Hoover Dam'.

The Year in Stats
Almost 100% of anything people do is now described online as courageous, uplifting or brave.

Wife enjoys last few days with husband before release Of *Fallout 4*

A Dublin woman has unveiled her poignant plans for her last few remaining days with her husband of ten years, before he slips into a PlayStation coma when the long-awaited video game *Fallout 4* is finally released.

Over the next fortnight, Helen Currie, 37, will spend as much time as she can engaging in activities with her husband Malcolm, such as talking and being outside, which will be impossible after he gets his hands on *Fallout 4*.

Fallout 4 is the latest in the long-running adventure saga from Bethesda Software and is due for release on 10 November. The series is known for its thrilling post-apocalyptic setting, addictive role-playing story, and its ability to render gamers unresponsive for months on end.

Following the release of *Fallout 3* in 2008, Malcolm Currie spent seven months in a near-vegetative state, responding to his wife only with grunts and the occasional raised eyebrow.

Fearing that she may not have a conversation with her husband until the middle of next year, Mrs Currie is soaking up as much time with him as possible.

'It's the little things I'll miss the most,' sighed Helen, fighting back tears. 'Things like him answering me when I ask him questions, or being in a standing position. Being off the sofa, basically. It'll all go out the window till November at the earliest.'

News that this edition of *Fallout* was by far the most ambitious in the series did little to soothe Mrs Currie, who broke down in floods of tears.

BREAKING NEWS

Do you have old VHS tapes in the attic? They could be worth fuck all!

Your decision to store all your old VHS tapes in the attic in the belief that one day they might be worth a fortune has finally been proven incorrect with the announcement that those things are worth fuck all, pal.

Studies have shown that even tapes with 'limited edition' or 'collector's item' written on them are worth less than the effort required to go out to the garage, get the ladder, go up through the little door into the attic, find the boxes marked 'tapes', haul those downstairs in stages, and sell them online.

Notions that your ex-rental copy of *Starship Troopers* would one day be 'worth a few quid' have not and will not come to fruition, and a spokesperson for people with a stack of tapes up in the attic confided in WWN that he and those like him now feel 'quite foolish'.

'I hate to say it, but my wife was right,' said Cathal McGahin, sifting through a mountain of videotapes. '*Predator 2*... this cost me £8, and now it's worth 100 per cent less than that. *The Full Monty*, *Thelma & Louise*, *Match of the Day* taped off the telly... all worth nothing. I should have thrown them out when I had the chance. With bin charges, I'm going to be down money.'

People upset about the current value of their VHS collections are advised not to look at how much their CDs are worth either.

Outrage at news that referendum on same-sex divorce will not be held until 2055

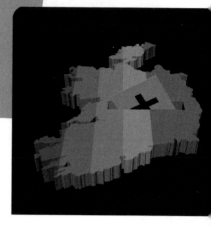

Despite nationwide celebrations among the LGBT community when the same-sex Marriage Act 2015 was passed, thousands of would-be couples will face a wait of almost forty years if they wish to get a divorce from their future partners.

Due to a previously overlooked clause, it transpires that married gay couples will not be able to divorce under the current constitution, forcing the government to announce a referendum for 22 May 2055.

'Unfortunately, the Fifteenth Amendment of the Constitution of Ireland, which had previously removed the constitutional prohibition of divorce in 1995, did not include gay marriage at the time and we now have to go through the whole process again,' a very worried-looking Taoiseach Enda Kenny explained outside Leinster House. 'This slight oversight will prevent same-sex couples from getting a divorce for now, but the good news is we have already organised a same-sex divorce referendum for 2055,' he continued, and closed by adding 'Sure, ye won't feel the time flying at'all.'

It is understood that opponents of the marriage referendum are already gearing up for #DivRef2055, printing thousands of 'No' flyers that will be posted to every household nationwide.

'We might as well get in there early,' said Irish teacher and opponent of the marriage referendum, Breda O'Brien. 'Let's see how long they can stick being married to someone they don't love any more, like us practising Catholics do. This will be the real test of their supposed love for one another.'

The Taoiseach has urged gay couples wishing to get married to make sure that they really mean it at the time, and not to jump into something they can't get out of for the next forty years.

BREAKING NEWS

Mick Wallace and Clare Daly drive off cliff in convertible while holding hands

It is with great sadness that WWN reports that sitting TDs Mick Wallace and Clare Daly drove their 1966 Ford Thunderbird off a cliff earlier this morning, as legions of Gardaí pursued the pair in their squad cars.

Kindred spirits in a world that seemed out of step with them, the Wexford and Dublin North TDs had found common ground on the issue of American warplanes landing and refuelling at Shannon airport.

In an attempt to break from their stilted and dreary existence, Wallace and Daly had taken a road trip to Shannon Airport last year, but after breaking the law there, the pair had been constantly pursued by the authorities.

After their escape from prison, the fugitives were finally cornered in Paulstown, Kilkenny, home to one of Ireland's largest quarries.

Resolving that a lifetime in prison for their heinous crimes was too much to take, Wallace, clad in a stylish headscarf to protect his hair from the unforgiving wind was overheard telling Daly they should just 'keep going'.

Holding hands over the car's gearbox, the TDs let go of the clutch together, and before Gardaí could act, the pair accelerated towards the edge of the quarry cliff only to become suspended in a freeze frame several feet over the edge, before it is believed they plummeted to their deaths.

Authorities have been unable to confirm if Wallace spent the previous night entangled in a lovemaking session with Brad Pitt.

The untold history of the Orange Order parades

With the Twelfth of July officially upon us, we look back at the little-known history of Orange Order parades, and how they came about.

The Loyal Orange Institution, more commonly known as the Orange Order, is a Protestant organisation based primarily in Northern Ireland. The order was founded in 1795 in a bid to bring some sort of order to the way fruit was being displayed in the many fruit stalls across the six counties.

The problem was that the poorer Catholic street traders would throw different varieties of fruit on to the same stall, with no separation between items, making it difficult for buyers to find what they wanted. Not only was the jumbled-up fruit unsightly, it also encouraged mould and rot to fester quite quickly, ruining the produce.

The Protestants, or 'protesting ants' as they were originally called, began feuding with the Catholics about their idiotic shelving, insisting the fruit should be separated.

On 12 July 1803, the Orange Order decided to make a stand, organising a march right through the heart of Belfast city and along the Shankill Road, where dozens of Catholic fruit sellers were based. Historians state that over three hundred Orange Order members marched down through the stalls, carefully separating apples from pears, bananas from oranges, and even arranging the fruit in order of ripeness. This upset the Catholics and violence soon broke out on the street. Several people on both sides were tragically killed.

Every year thereafter, the Orange Order insisted on repeating the OCD-based march in defiance of the Catholics' stance on fruit, with more and more people dying annually.

It wasn't until the Good Friday Agreement in 1998 that Catholics finally began sorting out their fruit stalls, and a peace treaty was signed.

Keeping with tradition, the Orange Order continues to march every year on the Twelfth of July to commemorate two centuries of fruit disorganisation. Even today, large pallets of fruit are still ritually burned, hopefully along with the disagreements between the two factions.

'I did it for Ireland,' claims Healy-Rae attacker

Kerry TD Michael Healy-Rae is said to be recovering well in hospital after a failed attempt on his life by a cow that Gardaí believe was radicalised by Dublin-based 'urban extremists'.

The cow, named locally as New Road Healy-Rae, was said to be troubled by the fact that its owner and his TD brother had taken outstpoken stances against Irish Water and auctions for distressed properties and then Michael Healy-Rae had proceeded to win Irish Water contracts and Danny Healy-Rae had purchased a property at an auction that he had previously vocally opposed.

'They're playing their voters and the nation for fools – I didn't do this for me; I did this for Ireland,' New Road told WWN.

'That sounds like a load of Dublin shite-talk,' Danny Healy-Rae responded when confronted by WWN about the cow's allegations. 'Some city slicker has got into her head, filling it with dreams about an organic milk café up in Dublin. Did you know she was calving at the time? She wasn't herself at all.'

The cow has strenuously denied being affiliated with any Dublin urban extremist groups such as Fine Gael, but reiterated that she felt she did the right thing.

'His flat cap came flying off and out spilled road construction contracts, signed off by the council his brother sat on at the time. It doesn't sound like rural affairs were at the centre of his thoughts – more like Healy-Rae affairs.'

The Kerry TD's exit from hospital is set to be delayed by several hours as the new road from the hospital to his front door has yet to be completed.

Doctors say Taoiseach 'doing well' after surgery to remove his head from his arse

Standing outside Denis O'Brien's privately owned Beacon Hospital earlier this morning, surgeon Michael Clark delivered the good news to an anxious public that their Taoiseach, Enda Kenny was doing well after the successful removal of his head from his arse.

The Taoiseach was rushed to hospital late yesterday evening after several suspect public utterances led a doctor watching the *Six One News* to diagnose the Taoiseach with a case of *Headious-up-arsesus*, a rare affliction which only affects 98 per cent of Irish politicians.

'I was watching the news and there was the Taoiseach saying he couldn't commit to climate-change-emissions targets, and I realised what was wrong instantly,' explained doctor and TV viewer Rebecca Drummond.

Headious-up-arsesus leaves the afflicted unable to perform basic tasks like putting the health of the nation and its environment ahead of a few farmers who might not vote for him if he pushes for a reduction in agri-sector pollution.

'Here was a guy saying the country couldn't commit to emission cuts due to economic circumstances, but it was clear he was putting rural votes in the upcoming election ahead of everything else. The worry was that his head had ascended so far up his anus that there would be no way of retrieving it,' Dr Drummond added.

After staff close to the Taoiseach were informed of the condition, they acted quickly and passed on the information to the Taoiseach himself, but not before he spoke out on homelessness stating there was 'no reason for anyone to be homeless this Christmas'. It was at this point that all involved knew it was a critical problem.

Surgery was delayed, however, when the Taoiseach refused to go to any public hospital on the grounds that 'they are death traps, and I wouldn't mind being seen some time within the next ten years'.

EXCLUSIVE

Government purchases new rug under which to sweep abortion problem

The government has announced the exclusive purchase of a new rug that is believed to be big enough to cover all the floors in Leinster House, effectively allowing government officials to sweep problems relating to Irish abortion laws under it.

'We had the lads out in IKEA at the start of the summer, but there's just so much choice, you know, it's hard to make a decision,' a government source told WWN.

'Our requirements were obviously very specific – this had to be a massive, massive rug. You can't just sweep this problem under any old thing. We'll get it installed before the Dáil is back in session so they don't have to answer any questions about it,' the source confirmed.

The purchase of the new rug is a progressive new strategy that perfectly compliments last year's moving ceremony during which the government handed over the responsibility for solving the constitutional conundrum to the next generation.

Rug experts believe the government has chosen Abortenprublen, one of IKEA's most popular rugs, and one that a number of families in Ireland already have in their homes. It is also believed that the government will have to staple several of these rugs together to properly cover everything up.

'Well obviously after telling the nation's youth "fuck it, you can sort it out down the line", we needed to stop everyone talking about this abortion stuff, and it is a lovely rug with plenty of room underneath it in fairness,' a Fine Gael TD told WWN.

Kexit:
what it will mean if Kerry leaves Ireland

Inspired by the political firepower of the Healy-Rae dynasty and believing itself to be far better off away from the Republic of Ireland, the county of Kerry is planning to go to the polls in the coming months to decide whether or not to break away from the state and form a country of its own.

Should this so-called Kexit take place, Ireland will be a very different place than it is today. Here are some things you need to know ahead of polling day:

1. The Healy-Raes will form a government

If Kerry leaves Ireland, no elections will take place to appoint a ruler of this new country. The Healy-Rae brothers, Michael and Danny, will remain in power in a two-person coalition. No opposition party will exist, and the rest of the ministerial roles such as those for transport and health will be given to other members of the Healy-Rae family.

2. Irish tourism will take a major hit

Ireland heavily relies on revenue from tourism. With the Ring of Kerry now in a different country, Ireland will need to create new attractions to draw tourists away from the country of Kerry. Plans to renovate Glendalough have already been drafted up.

3. Kerry will abolish several archaic laws

Free from hassle from 'them smart boys up in Dublin', Kerry will be free to finally abolish restrictive laws such as 'Don't drink and drive'. Road deaths may soar in the following months but at least Kerry people will be free.

4. Puck Fair will happen once a month

The contentious Puck Fair, along with the crowning of a goat as King Puck, will go from taking place once a year to happening on the the first Friday of every month. 'We'll put as many goats up on scaffolding as we like,' said one pro-Kexit campaigner.

5. The punt will be re-established

Free to create its own currency, the country of Kerry will bring the punt back into circulation. The late Jackie Healy-Rae will adorn the 10 pound note. One Kerry punt will be worth 20c.

6. Dublin will win the All-Ireland for the next twenty years

With no Kerry team to beat them, the Dubs will sweep to victory at every All-Ireland GAA championship for the next two decades.

Government urging homeless people not to die so close to the Dáil

Minister for the Environment Alan Kelly has today called on members of the homeless community to try to stay clear of Leinster House if they feel like they're about to die.

Speaking to WWN this morning, Mr Kelly urged people who are on the verge of passing over to think about their government and the consequences of their chosen location, as dying on the doorstep of the country's main government building is 'bad form', especially given the upcoming election.

'I'm not saying they're doing it on purpose,' he said, referring to the four homeless people that have died in the last month in close proximity to the Dáil. 'It just looks bad on the government if they keep doing it. There is no shortage of places to die around Dublin city, thanks to the hard work of this government.'

Hinting at more disadvantaged areas like the north inner city, Mr Kelly suggested that those who feel close to death should pick more suitable surroundings.

'There are plenty of derelict buildings around the city that people can die in,' he added. 'If I was homeless, I'd certainly not want to be seen making a show of my country. I'd die with dignity in a disused warehouse or something so as not to cause a fuss.'

Yesterday, another body of a man was found by a member of the public on Dawson Lane just off Dawson Street at approximately 7 a.m., where it is believed he had been sleeping rough for some time.

Gardaí do not suspect foul play, despite an additional 700 people being left homeless on Irish streets since the Fine Gael/Labour party government came to power in 2014.

YEAR IN REVIEW

Bills proposed in Dáil Éireann this year that failed to pass

Make Every Day 1916 Commemoration Day Bill 2016 (proposed by Sinn Féin TD Gerry Adams)

· · · · ·

Leo Varadkar Should Be Taoiseach Cos He's Real Cool & Stuff Bill 2016 (proposed by Fine Gael TD Leo Varadkar)

· · · · ·

Ah, Ease Up On All This Receiving Money From Rich Businessmen Bill 2016 (proposed by independent TD Michael Lowry)

· · · · ·

Let's Do Something About The 8th Amendment Shall We? Bill 2016 (proposed by anyone except the government)

· · · · ·

TDs With Long Hair And Pink T-shirts Should Be Forced To Clean Themselves Up Bill 2016 (proposed by former Fine Gael TD Alan Shatter)

· · · · ·

The Solving The Housing Crisis But Only If It Lines The Pockets Of The Developers Bill 2016 (joint proposal by Fianna Fáil TD Micheál Martin and Fine Gael TD Enda Kenny)

· · · · ·

The Give Kerry Loadsa Money Bill 2016 (joint proposal by independent TDs Michael Healy-Rae, Danny Healy-Rae, Johnny Healy-Rae, Jimmy Healy-Rae, Tommy Healy-Rae, Billy Healy-Rae, Ray Healy-Rae, Michael Healy-Rae Jr and Michael Healy-Rae Jr Jr)

IRA formally denies it still exists

In a press conference at a secret location in Antrim, leading spokesmen for the Irish Republican Army have today formally denied that the organisation still exists.

Slamming a damning joint PSNI-MI5 report that claims IRA members are still operating, a spokesman flanked by four masked members said the accusations were false and politically motivated, and not to trust everything you see, hear or read.

'It's all lies,' the uniformed IRA member explained. 'There are no paramilitaries here anymore. Everyone has moved on with their lives and they have proper jobs, paying tax to the Queen and all hi!'

During the eight-minute address, the speaker picked up a handgun from the table and fired shots into the air, sending plaster down on people's heads. The group claimed it was their last bullet and told the public not to worry any more about violence, drug-running, racketeering or fuel laundering.

'See, that there was our last lucky bullet which we kept for the craic hi,' he added, emptying the shell from the chamber and dusting off his shoulders. 'Now we're defenceless altogether, see? The old days are gone – no need to panic. This whole PSNI-MI5 report is just a bunch of old wives' tales to make children go to sleep. If you could smell the mould from these uniforms you'd believe us. The stink of them – haven't been worn in years.'

The IRA's confirmation that it doesn't exist anymore appears to have temporarily defused a political crisis at Stormont, alleviating many DUP members' fears about the peace process.

'We're glad the IRA finally came out of the woodwork to deny its existence,' a DUP statement said. 'Hopefully we can all go back to normal, until the next Irish General Election, when they will need us again to prove more links between Sinn Féin and the IRA.'

Financial pearls of wisdom from Economics Correspondent Freddy Nobbs

Reinvest the €2 euro you win on scratch cards in TWO €1 euro scratch cards. No-nonsense financial sense.

Reports of clowns in Leinster House

Following an eerie outbreak of clown sightings across the world in recent weeks, Ireland has joined the list of countries where the creepy figures have appeared, with reports suggesting that large numbers of them have been spotted in Leinster House.

The strange phenomenon was first reported in America, where a number of kids made claims that people dressed as clowns had tried to lure them into the woods with sweets and cash.

Copycat sightings spread across the States and were followed by similar reports from the UK and mainland Europe, with details scarce as to who was behind the prank or their motives.

However, the news that clowns have been spotted in the Irish houses of parliament is especially noteworthy due to the high number that have been sighted in a single location, with one eyewitness claiming that there were up to 158 clowns on the premises.

'You see them from time to time, skulking around in the shadows,' said Eoin Lavery, who drew attention to the spooky sightings.

'Men, women, young, old ... just a mix of these creepy-looking ghoulish clowns. Some of them saw us and tried to lure us to them with promises of fixing roads and cutting taxes, but we knew it was a trick and kept our distance.'

If any of these clowns should come to your door or post a leaflet through your letterbox, please ignore them completely.

All these fools gonna make me bust my nine, confirms Adams

Sinn Féin leader Gerry Adams has issued a statement in which he justifies his use of the N-word by claiming that he has 'never really identified as white', adding that 'any of you honky mothers that don't get that' may be candidates for a date with 'his nine'.

Adams made the latest statement while chilling in his crib with his homies, following a weekend spent explaining himself after posting a tweet about the movie *Django Unchained*.

Making the point that being a Catholic living in Northern Ireland was similar to being an African–American living in the USA, the tweet caused international outrage among the Irish media, who called on Adams to explain himself dozens of times.

Having had enough, Adams took to YouTube with a video message for 'da haters', in which he made thinly veiled threats to 'bust a cap in yo ass'.

'Y'all thinking this a game, bitch? I'm the realest motherfucker ever to come out the hood in Ballymurphy,' said Adams, while pointing a Glock pistol sideways at the camera.

'This beef ends here. Me and my whole crew gonna run up on you if you be dissing the Sinn Féin posse. Real talk. Adams out.'

Adams later denied having a 'nine', or indeed knowing anyone who had ever used one.

'It's broadband or no flooding – you can't have both,' culchies told

The government has been unequivocal in its response to criticism of their handling of recent flooding, with ministers revealing culchies just can't have everything they bloody well want.

With extensive flooding in Kilkenny, Cork, Wexford, and other places that aren't Dublin, the government confirmed that an ultimatum has been delivered to the nation's culchies.

'It's fairly straightforward really – either we stop the flooding, but you get no broadband; or keep the flooding, but on the plus side ye lot have some broadband,' Taoiseach

Enda Kenny revealed while visiting the scene of a puddle outside Leinster House this morning.

In a separate interview, Minister for the Environment Alan Kelly laid out the reality of the situation: 'There's no money in the culchie budget, which is distinct from the Dublin budget, so really just ask yourselves, do ya want broadband or not? 'Cos access to funny online videos doesn't fall out of the sky, ya know,' the minister explained.

The choice between putting money towards a cohesive flooding strategy that comes into effect before the event may be tempting for flood-hit

areas, but choosing such an option at the expense of quick and easy access to the internet and online pornography has divided the rural community.

'Jesus, I don't know now. I mean I have the broadband, and it's shite altogether, but every so often I can get a glimpse of something … and the thought of giving that up … I think I'd rather convert the downstairs into an indoor swimming pool,' shared flood victim and broadband lover Fergus Varley.

The government has asked that culchies vote on the matter sometime later this week.

Michael D. Higgins captured by person playing Pokémon GO

The search is on for Irish President Michael D. Higgins, who is believed to have been captured in Phoenix Park by someone playing the new augmented-reality phone game Pokémon GO.

The incredibly popular new app allows players to 'look' for Pokémon in the real world, and has been downloaded millions of times since its launch earlier this year.

It is believed that an over-eager player who parked close to Áras an Uachtaráin may have mistaken a passing President Higgins for one of the game's scruffy little monster characters, before launching a Pokéball at him and sucking him into the game.

The hunt is now on to find President Higgins before he is forced to go one-on-one with a Charizard, a contest which Pokémon experts claim he has 'no chance' of winning.

'It'll be a case of "Higgins used poetry… It's not very effective",' said one 47-year-old man who is way too old to be playing Pokémon. 'So you'd better find out who has him, and quick. Best case scenario would be if he didn't battle, and was just left to evolve into Higginstwo, but I'm not sure I'd want something like that running the country.'

Luckily for President Higgins, the Pokémon GO app has been crashing since its launch, meaning the chances of anyone actually being able to battle against him are non-existent at this point.

Danny Healy-Rae suggests leaving Child of Prague under bush to combat climate change

Although Danny Healy-Rae is standing by his comments that 'only God above is in charge of the weather', the Kerry TD has admitted that Ireland can tackle climate change by implementing some tried-and-tested methods such as leaving a statue of the Child of Prague under a bush overnight.

Healy-Rae was speaking at a climate change discussion in the Dáil recently, when he made the argument that carbon taxation aimed at curbing climate change was costing the rural community massive sums of money.

Arguing against some fairly significant data mined from surveys and scientific research from all over the world, Healy-Rae stressed that there wasn't much that a government could do about climate change, but conceded that he would get as many people in his constituency to put their Child of Prague out in the ditch, and encourage them to have their St Brigid's cloak to hand at all times.

'You can't change the climate of the world by addressing carbon emissions or listening to scientists,' said Healy-Rae, eating a Caramac. 'But we'll do our best to ensure a few grand nice days there with the Child of Prague under the hedge. Sure didn't it work for us there in Kerry the time we were going to our cousin's wedding? We put the statue out and it was a fierce day the next day altogether. There's no reason a concentrated effort by a few hundred thousand people across the country couldn't do more for climate change than you'd ever get done by banning fossil fuels.'

Healy-Rae went on to state that the plan faced opposition 'up in Dublin', adding, 'they're just mad that they live in flats and don't have a hedge to call their own.'

Government to hand out free hangers to women who can't afford trip to England

In order to ward off any attempt by Repeal the 8th campaigners to press for a referendum on abortion in Ireland, the government has launched an innovative and forward-thinking initiative which could serve as an alternative to an expensive trip to England.

The government has made a bulk purchase of over two million clothes hangers that will be sent out to every female Irish citizen, in the event that they might need or desire an abortion.

'We just couldn't be arsed going through the stress of a referendum, plus it's a matter of conscience and all that, so we're sending off the hangers, and we'll let people's consciences do the rest,' explained a government spokesman as he placed hangers into individual envelopes, earmarked for the women and girls of Ireland.

'And yes, it does get to us that some women have been priced out of abortions in England due to the associated costs – it's a disgrace. We knew we had to do something about it here on a governmental level, and so the nationwide hangers distribution plan was born,' added the spokesman.

While the envelopes won't carry precise instructions, the government is trusting that the women of Ireland are well read on alternative methods of termination at this stage, in the absence of real access to healthcare.

'It's a gentle and understanding tightrope we're balancing on here. We don't want to be seen to condone things like abortion, but if women find themselves in desperate circumstances, where the hangers could be an option, then who are we to deny them,' a spokesperson for the Irish Commission On Things We Don't Talk About (ICOTWDTA) explained.

The ICOTWDTA spokesperson pointed out that although many women will feel they have no need for the hanger, they can hold on to it and pass it on as a gift to future generations of Irish women.

We spend a day with the Healy-Raes

WWN's editor and chief political reporter Paddy Browne travelled to Kerry earlier this week to secure a rare interview with the media-shy Healy-Rae TDs. Delving deep into the Healy-Rae mythos, Paddy learned all about their political successes and plans for the future.

Ensconced deep in the wilds of Kerry, embedded in roadside bush, I wait, hopeful for an encounter with the esteemed princes of Kerry, Michael and Danny Healy-Rae.

Thanks to a tip-off from a local constituent, I know that both Healy-Rae brothers regularly parade around Kerry on newly tarmacked roads, waving from the comfort of their cars, much like the Queen of England does when visiting her loyal subjects.

A battered 1979 Ford Mondeo chugs along the road – could it be one of the TDs? All doubt was removed from my mind when both men came into view wearing paddy caps on their heads and their arms and their shoulders. It was them all right.

Aware of how hostile Michael and Danny can be towards the media I jumped out on the road and shouted, 'I have a local government road contract to give you.' A screech of brakes and the men exited the car. Once they were within my sights, I handcuffed both of them to myself and suggested we got to know each other.

They point-blank refused, citing my 'posh inner-city Waterford accent' and the fact I was a journalist as proof that I shouldn't be trusted.

'Sure, you rich folk up in the castles and mansions in Waterford city only look down on us poor Kerrymen. You'd probably be there laffing about how you all have nine jobs each while there's families eating one another down here to

get just one job between twelve of them, because the big boys up in the Dublin political mafia don't care,' Michael shared, his sharp eyes full of hatred for my modern and sophisticated Waterford city ways.

Out of nowhere, hundreds of locals rose from the high grass on the hillside to clap Michael's anti-Dublin hate speech and to spit on me.

Thinking on my feet, I decided to play up my accent, and the two TDs seemed to open up to me the more country and culchie I sounded. Soon I found myself just grunting and banging rocks off my head, and Michael and Danny's glares turned to warm expressions of friendship. They had misjudged me, they admitted. I responded by delivering a calf from a nearby cow and then eating my own faeces. They were suddenly at ease – I was 'one of them'.

Reassured that we could talk as friends, I released them from their handcuffs and they agreed to bring me back to 'Healy country', the heartland of their political revolution. We circled the Ring of Kerry for nine hours. Danny sat with his head out the window, tongue hanging out, lapping up the air like a dog for the entire journey, and with a pen in his hand. Every mile or so we'd encounter someone with a new contract for some new local project which Danny would sign at speed and then confirm one of his forty-nine companies would begin work on the next day.

After changing direction countless times on the roads, we arrived at the humble HQ – a small sodden cottage with a turf roof stood at the end of a road. The structure seemed very unstable and leaned over to one side. It couldn't have been any bigger than a small dog and yet it was home to both Michael and Danny Healy-Rae's families.

'Tis not for Dublin folk at all, but we're a modest sort. I live here with

Soon the Healy-Raes were kings of Kerry, despite coming from good Anglo-French stock and their name originally being Hailée-Yves. They swept up all before them, tightening their grip on Irish politics.

I was still trying to digest all this new information when I was shown around the scientific research wing of the Healy compound. Endless tubes containing naked men bearing a striking resemblance to Michael and Danny were on display.

'The plan is that by 2020 we will have a Healy-Rae clone running in each and every constituency in Ireland. Each clone will be uniquely suited to the necessary culchie stereotype needed for any given constituency,' Michael explained as he observed his team of Harvard-educated scientists working on the latest DNA strands.

'Kerry was just the beginning – tomorrow the world,' Michael said menacingly, just shortly before Danny struck me over the head with a block of posh cheese of a variety you can only get up in Dublin.

I later awoke in the same roadside bush I'd started my day in, only this time I was naked, and spray-painted on my body were the words 'go back to posh and rich Waterford ya townie bastard'. I had been played; I had been well and truly Healy-Rayed.

my ten childer,' Michael began to explain. 'Danny's here with his nineteen childer, and then we have the cousins, and the aunts, and the uncles. It's eight people to a bed, and we like it fine, even if the uppity folk in Dublin wouldn't understand.'

At Michael's insistence, I entered the small structure through the 11-inch-high front door. It was a struggle, but I pushed on through and that was when things took a sinister turn.

Once safely inside the miniscule house, Michael took off all seventeen of his flat caps, and his speech improved dramatically. In fact, he began sounding like someone who actually had a grasp of the English language.

'How d'ya like the gaff, man?' Michael queried as I looked around for the first time with Michael's new and abrasive Dublin 4 accent ringing in my ears.

'Fuckin' sweet digs or what?' added Danny, who had magically regrown all the teeth missing from his mouth.

The modest Healy-Rae residence I had seen from the outside was just window dressing, a cover for an expansive compound the like of which I'd never seen before. Grand and majestic houses in the latest modern architectural style sat alongside vast garages filled to the brim with Ferraris, Bentleys

and Maseratis. Massive TV screens played French art-house movies and rugby matches.

Still shell-shocked, I asked Michael what exactly I was witnessing here.

'The greatest trick a jackeen ever pulled – convincing a culchie he was one of them,' Michael said as a butler emerged from nowhere to hand him a 1969 Sauvignon Blanc.

'My father, God rest him, was Foxrock-born-and-bred, but like, the political game there was totes fierce and unforgiving so he like, hatched a plan to move to Kerry and build a political dynasty there,' Danny chimed in.

'He just rocked up here one day and when anyone questioned who he was, he said, "I'm from the Kerry Healy-Raes." He knew country folk would lose face if they admitted to having not heard of someone living locally so he got away with it.'

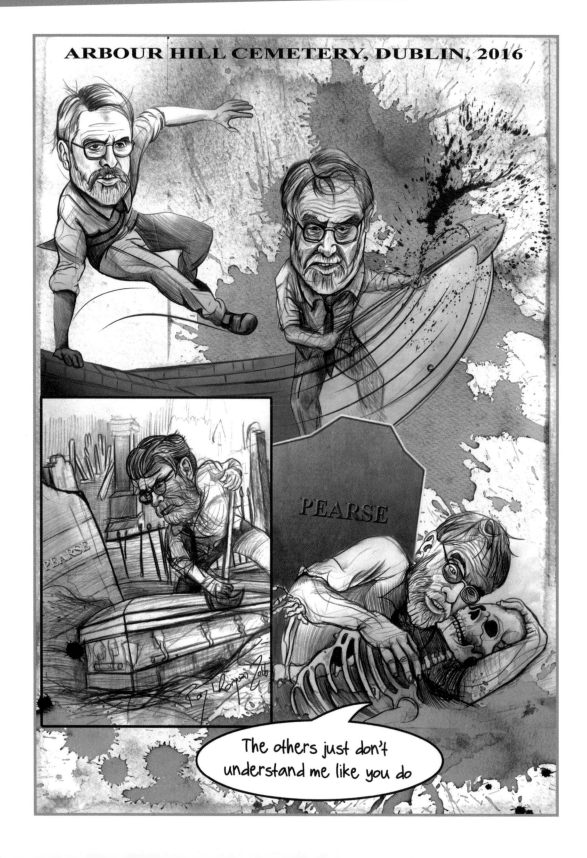

ELECTION SPECIAL

GET YOURSELF A BIG MUG OF VODKA AND JOIN WWN AS WE RELIVE THE MAGIC OF THE IRISH ELECTION

Government announces 30 February election date

Taoiseach Enda Kenny finally confirmed the date of the General Election at Áras an Uachtaráin earlier this morning. Speaking outside the presidential residence, Mr Kenny thanked everyone for their patience, and apologised for delaying the announcement until now, blaming internal factors in the coalition government.

'Following a lengthy debate between the Labour party and Fine Gael, I am delighted to announce the 2016 General Election will be held on Tuesday 30 February,' he said, to the flutter of press-camera flashes. 'We would have called this election sooner if it wasn't for everyone asking me all the time. I hate when people pressure me like that; it usually makes me wait out of spite. So, don't do that again.'

Unveiling a rather large February calendar to a very brief fireworks display, Mr Kenny seemingly struggled to find the date on the timeline, and quickly covered the calendar again.

'This calendar is obviously broken, but never mind that, we would encourage every Irish citizen over the age of eighteen to register and vote at the end of the month,' he said, before concluding, 'Who knows, we might even throw in an extra Bank Holiday this year ... or even an extra day if ye're good.'

Commuter settles on electoral candidate after seeing 783rd identical poster

A previously undecided voter has settled on his candidate of choice for the forthcoming General Election, after driving past the 783rd consecutive poster on his way to work.

Marcus Harkin, currently living in the Dublin South West constituency, hadn't previously had any intention of voting for his local Labour candidate Fergus Mullally until this morning's commute. Mullally's cheerful poster and inspiring 'Vote for Fergus Mullally' slogan finally convinced Harkin that this candidate was the man to hold one of the top positions in the country.

Experts believe that what Mr Harkin experienced today was the 'election poster effect', which candidates around the country rely on to sway undecided voters. Statistics are unclear as to exactly how many posters are needed to break through to the public, but it seems anything in the high hundreds is a good start.

'Cllr Mullally had two posters on every lamppost for three miles straight. The first 782 posters – I passed no remark on them,' said Harkin, speaking exclusively to WWN. 'But when I saw the 783rd, that's when it hit me – yeah, "vote for Mullally"... that has a real nice ring to it. So I'm going to vote for him at the end of the month. I don't need to see his policies or his road-fixing track record – he's got the most posters and that's what really matters.'

The news has spurred on politicians in the area to renew their efforts to erect thousands more posters over the next fortnight, while well-meaning candidates who are probably ideal for office but can only afford a hundred posters or so have been advised to stop wasting their time.

Gerry Adams lights IRA signal into sky from roof of Sinn Féin offices

Despite the Dublin skyline being thick with fog, an unmistakable and long-absent sight dominated everyone's view as it made its return to the skies.

The IRA signal, a beacon used by members of Sinn Féin in times past if they needed help from the paramilitary organisation, scorched the skies once more – and attracted the interest of nearby Gardaí – as Sinn Féin's leader Gerry Adams took to the roof of his party's offices.

It is believed Adams activated the supposedly dormant signal as he is in urgent need of help following the rejection of Sinn Féin by almost 100 per cent of the country's other left-leaning political parties as well as a growing weariness among some voters.

However, Sinn Féin issued a press release some four minutes before Adams took to the roof to switch on the IRA signal, denying he had done such a thing.

'We saw him with our own eyes for Christ's sake,' responding Gardaí told Sinn Féin members in the party's offices, but Gardaí were reminded that Adams was fond of doing things 'just for shits and giggles'.

'Ah sure, that thing is always malfunctioning,' Adams explained to Gardaí after descending from the rooftop. 'To the untrained eye, it would appear as if the signal has never been properly switched off, but the roof is just where I go to do my thinking,' added the party leader.

ELECTION SPECIAL

'Anti-politician' bars installed outside homes across Ireland

The installation of 'anti-politician' bars outside homes across the country has been welcomed by many as a small step towards curbing the scourge of finding unwanted Dáil members at your door.

The idea for installing the bars came after it emerged that council workers had erected 'anti-homeless' barriers on ledges outside the offices of the Department of Social Protection in Dublin's city centre.

Impressed with the bluntness of the government's attitude towards the most vulnerable members of society, people all over Ireland have tweaked the idea and used it to deter doorstep canvassers during the coming General Election campaign.

Ranging from devices similar to large cattle grids, to sharp outward-facing metal spikes at shin level, these bars leave canvassers unable to ring a doorbell or post pamphlets through the front door of a house.

'Here, we see a series of 18-inch metal spikes at a 45-degree angle, situated about a metre from the door,' said Cathal Harris, an extremely busy anti-politician bar installer. 'So whoever lands at your door, say it's a member of the current government for example, perhaps someone who uses the government offices where the anti-homeless bars are currently in use ... say one of them lands at your door, well, they get an ankle-ful of spike and off they go.'

In locations where people were not able to install anti-politician spikes outside their homes, Harris suggested that the old-fashioned verbal method of forcefully telling politicians to leave your doorstep could be used as an alternative.

Increasingly desperate Fianna Fáil refuses to rule out coalition with ISIS

Fianna Fáil's profound desire to return to a position of power at all costs has seen the political party refuse to rule out a coalition with heinous terrorists ISIS, WWN has learned.

'I'm not going to say who we are or who we aren't willing to go into a coalition with,' Fianna Fáil leader Micheál Martin told reporters earlier today, deflecting direct questions about rumours of a power-sharing government with ISIS.

'Each individual party and organisation is very different, but we would of course listen to all offers,' Martin added as the sweat began to build on his brow.

While Fianna Fáil features in a number of political polls, the party is hated by vast swathes of the voting public, which has led senior members of the party to consider absolutely all and any offers of potential coalitions.

'Is terrorism bad? Yes. Are we interested in slowly creeping our way back into power when no one is looking? Yes. So you can see that in some cases, some coalition offers are problematic,' Martin confirmed to WWN.

Martin denied rumours that he now regularly watches the Al Jazeera news and that he has typed 'ISIS phone number' into Google.

Islanders think they're fucking great voting a day early

Voting in the 2016 General Election has already begun for thousands of smug islanders off the coast of Ireland.

Residents of a dozen or so islands off the coast of Donegal, Galway and Mayo began casting their ballots this morning, lording it over the remainder of the nation who won't get to the polls until tomorrow.

'They think they're fucking great,' pointed out one mainlander, who was too upset to say anything else.

Island dwellers traditionally vote a day ahead of everyone else, to prevent their votes being delayed from reaching the mainland due to bad weather and potentially holding up the count. However, this tradition is now outdated following the invention of things like telephones, meaning that islanders are only voting early so they can feel like big shots while the rest of the population waits around.

'Ah yeah, great to have the aul voting over and done with, isn't it?' said one Arranmore native. 'You know, just got up today, went down to the polling station and had a good hard vote. Great stuff altogether. I'd hate to have to wait another twenty-four hours – that would be terrible altogether. Imagine! Having to wait that long to vote! I feel so bad for anyone that hasn't voted yet.'

As the islands continue to have their say in the 2016 General Election, the rest of the nation is praying to God for a good big storm to hit the Atlantic coast.

The Year in Stats

77% of people able to cheer themselves up with a massive bitching session.

ELECTION SPECIAL

How to draw the perfect penis on your ballot paper

Fine Gael unveils giant 'Gerry was in the Ra' posters as election turns nasty

The underhand campaign tactics used by all major parties running in the election have reached a bitter low today as Fine Gael spent the last of their election war chest on a series of giant 'Gerry was in the Ra – Vote Fine Gael' posters.

Prospective voters woke today to find a number of the country's most famous landmarks draped in posters alluding to Gerry Adams' involvement in the IRA.

The Cliffs of Moher, the Spire, Newgrange, the Aviva Stadium and Thomond Park were just some of the landmarks covered in the incendiary posters from the majority coalition partner. It is believed that Fine Gael hopes this subtle reminder will push people away from voting for Sinn Féin.

'Honestly, we haven't a notion what you're talking about,' protested Fine Gael's director of elections Brian Hayes, as he stood in front of a freshly erected ninety-foot tall poster on the Rock of Cashel.

Motorists on the M50 had to drive under distracting conditions as Fine Gael had invested a significant amount re-laying the roads last night with 'Gerry was in the Ra' posters. Several hundred people have been injured in crashes as a result.

The posters also adorn the facades of the Empire State building, the Eiffel Tower, the Taj Mahal and the Egyptian pyramids and have attracted widespread international attention.

Sinn Féin has responded by tattooing homeless people with 'Official Fine Gael Policy' on the forehead and with a provocative 'Enda Kenny was not in the Ra – Vote Sinn Féin' poster.

As part of WWN's extensive coverage of the 2016 General Election we are addressing the issue of spoiling your vote.

Many disgruntled and disillusioned voters will choose to visit a polling station today only to spoil their vote. Political commentators see it as a controversial step to take, citing the act as a slight on those who fought to bring freedom to Ireland.

However, fiercer criticism has been directed at so-called 'spoilers' in recent times due to the decline in artistry in their work and the high volume of hasty scribbles on the ballots.

'There is a real lack of effort put into penis-based drawing on ballot papers these days,' remarked Ciaran Dunne, lecturer at NCAD in Dublin. 'While I'm not politically motivated myself I can't stand by and see someone crudely draw a penis and leave out pubic hair – it's disgraceful and lazy."

Dunne is not the only one who has made his displeasure known at the current standard of spoiling, as veteran vote-counter Mary Boland told WWN.

'I used to look forward to seeing them,' explained the 89-year-old. 'You know the big veiny ones were great – they'd break up the day nicely and in my younger days I used to sneak a few home for, well, you know yourself,' the feisty pensioner added.

NCAD lecturer Dunne outlined guidelines for WWN on how to draw the perfect penis on your ballot paper.

'To achieve optimum GBW – that's a "great big willy" to those who don't know – you must start with the shaft. Shaft is key. I cannot stress this enough. Make use of the entire page, obviously, and for the love of God do not neglect the balls. The number of times I've seen some truly beautiful portraits of shafts and heads only to see limp, half-arsed miniscule balls – it's heartbreaking.'

Dunne also stressed the importance of practising before going into the polling station and of not rushing the drawing once you are in there.

Dunne is running a penis portrait workshop all day today in an effort to increase the quality of spoiled votes this voting day.

Alan Kelly still celebrating on shoulders of campaign staff

Campaign staff for Alan Kelly are to continue parading him around 'in shifts', even after two people were admitted to Clonmel hospital with back and shoulder pain following a five-day celebration.

Speaking at a school sports hall in Tipperary, campaign manager Tony Hunt said he was delighted that Alan Kelly had retained his seat, but is looking forward to a break when the Labour Party politician finally stops celebrating.

'We've been here for the last 126 hours now and there is still no sign of him stopping,' a rather tired-looking Mr Hunt said. 'The school here has been very kind to us, but they are insisting we leave fairly soon as they've had to cancel all their PE classes this week due to Alan's celebrations.'

Still screaming at the top of his lungs and beating his chest, Alan Kelly shooed this reporter out of his way, whilst encouraging those carrying him on their backs to throw him even higher into the air.

'Do you see that, haters?' he shouted at our photographer, squeezing his left nipple with his right hand. 'Argh... never doubt the power of the Kelly! Kelly is king.'

Dropping in some lunch, Mr Kelly's wife Regina O'Connor said she was delighted for her husband, but that she looked forward to the day when he would finally settle down after his win.

'*House of Cards* will be back soon with a new season, thank God,' she said. 'It's the only thing that helps calm him down. That and drowning kittens.'

'You'll always be my Taoiseach,' Ted tells Adams

In a secluded corner of a Louth counting centre, a sad and moving election moment unfolded between Sinn Féin President Gerry Adams and his beloved teddy bear Ted.

Not long after being told by senior Sinn Féin election staff that some exit polls had placed the party at 16 per cent of the popular vote, the realisation that he would not be Taoiseach slowly dawned on Adams.

'Ted, Ted, what I am going to do with all those Taoiseach Gerry t-shirts I got printed up?' an emotional Adams asked his teddy bear as he sunk to his knees in a quiet corner. 'Snap Printing won't take them back, will they? Jesus, of course they won't. Stupid Gerry, *stupid Gerry*,' a frustrated Adams added, now slapping his forehead repeatedly.

It was then, in his moment of need, after a long and arduous campaign that had left Adams tired and unable to perform basic maths, that his treasured teddy bear addressed the Sinn Féin leader.

'You'll always be my Taoiseach,' Ted tenderly told Gerry, adding a wink for good effect. 'And don't worry about Slab. We'll make them all pay for Slab, every single last one of those bastards.'

'Aw, Ted, you always know what to say,' Gerry added as both Ted and Gerry began to quietly chant 'Taoiseach Gerry' over and over again to themselves.

ELECTION SPECIAL

Labour stock up on arse pads to avoid damage from door on way out

The 37 members of the Labour party who currently hold seats in the Dáil have begun raising funds for high-strength buttock pads, to lessen the damage to their gluteal area when the heavy doors of Leinster House hit them on their way out.

Opinion polls carried out during the current election campaign have shown that support for the party has plummeted, with many believing that Joan Burton and company face a near total wipe-out when the country goes to the polls this Friday.

Following the advice of the Green Party, who experienced a similar annihilation and severe door-related arse injuries following the 2011 General Election, Labour TDs are hoping to minimise the damage to their derrières by wearing specially designed pads.

Worn underneath their clothes, the pads will act as cushions for the outgoing TDs and will bear the brunt of the impact as the doors hit them on their way to the dole queue.

'If only I'd worn them when I was leaving, I would still be able to walk,' said Derek Manning, a former Green Party TD who was paralysed from the waist down when the doors of Leinster House smacked him on the arse in 2011. 'My advice to Joan and the rest of them is to take all necessary precautions to ensure they don't suffer like I did. If they can't find suitable butt guards, then improvise; stuff a load of newspaper or kitchen roll down there, anything at all, just don't go unprotected.'

Meanwhile, at Leinster House, staff members have begun oiling the hinges of the front door to make sure it gives each and every outgoing TD the whack they deserve.

Outgoing Labour and Fine Gael TDs told there's always JobBridge

High-profile Labour and Fine Gael casualties of the 2016 General Election have been inundated with correspondence from thoughtful members of the public who are trying to help the former TDs get a foot back on the employment ladder, WWN has learned.

James Reilly, Alan Shatter, Alex White, Kathleen Lynch, Ciaran Lynch, Jimmy Deenihan and Jerry Buttimer were among the coalition election casualties and once a new government is formed, they face the prospect of being out of a job.

However, in a heartwarming turn of events, large numbers of the Irish public have informed the outgoing TDs of a rewarding internship scheme called JobBridge.

'It's tough when you lose a job and I genuinely wouldn't wish it on anyone. That's why I'm writing to you,' began one piece of correspondence sent to Alan Shatter and seen by WWN. The email went on: 'There's a newsagents around the corner from me that has a nine-month position for a chief breakfast roll technician. I know what you're thinking, Alan – you don't have the experience, but if you don't put yourself up for these sorts of things, you've only yourself to blame.'

This rather uncommon outpouring of empathy for exiting TDs is perhaps an indication that the public is slowly beginning to develop an appreciation for their public representatives.

'Ah, they won't be on the couch for long, just look at these jobs,' explained Head of JobBridge Coordination Dermot Dolan: 'Nine month internship, psychologist, minimum five years experience; nightclub bouncer, seven months, minimum experience of three violent assaults. And while the pay works out at about €1.50 an hour, you can't put a price on the experience they're getting.'

Fianna Fáil voters wondering how Americans voting for Trump can be so stupid

Thousands of Irish people who voted for Fianna Fáil in the recent General Election have taken to social media to ridicule and criticise American people who are in favour of Donald Trump's campaign to be the President of the United States.

Trump's race to earn the Republican nomination for the presidency took a giant leap forward yesterday, with huge victories in the 'Super Tuesday' series of primaries.

This led to people across the world voicing their disbelief as to how someone like Trump can garner such support, including posts from Irish people who voted in their thousands for the same political party that brought about a generation of unemployment and austerity only a few short years ago.

'They're some thicks, them Americans,' said one man we spoke to, who last Friday gave his Number 1 vote to Micheál Martin.

'They don't seem to see Trump for the sneaky bastard that he is, and are just getting swept up in his speeches and how he endlessly creates scapegoats for everything that's wrong with the country, before promising to be the quick fix to sort everything out. I'll tell you, if there was any politician like that in Ireland, there's no way I'd vote for him.'

Meanwhile, Trump's rivals in the race for nomination are starting to wonder if they should start aligning themselves with the KKK to try and win some of that sweet Trump support.

Public disappointed that hung Dáil doesn't mean what they think it means

The Irish people were today told to temper their excitement as news agencies were forced to issue statements clarifying that when they say it's looking like a hung Dáil, it doesn't mean anything like what you might hope it does.

The nation took to the polls this morning in one of the most hotly contested elections in recent years, with exit polls showing that Labour may not be able to win enough seats to maintain a coalition with Fine Gael.

That would leave Fine Gael with no other choice but to partner up with Fianna Fáil, something both parties have strenuously refused to consider.

Should no coalition be formed, the country could be forced into a second General Election after the declaration of a 'hung Dáil' which does not mean that every single TD is dragged into the streets and hung from the nearest lamppost. Clarification of the term 'hung Dáil' came as thousands of citizens had begun to celebrate on the streets while making their way to Leinster House, and has dampened the spirits of the crowd considerably.

'Ah, it means what?' moaned one citizen we spoke to, as the carnival atmosphere died down. 'I thought these robbing, lying bastards were finally going to get what they deserve. I took a half-day off work for this, and I went out and bought a brand new rope.'

The electorate was also upset to find that 'the party whip' is not what they thought it was either.

ELECTION SPECIAL

Bizarre scenes as Joan Burton's eyes roll back and she begins chanting 'join us'

Former Tánaiste Joan Burton has been asked by the Ceann Comhairle to clarify what she meant when she told the TDs in the Dáil chamber that they should 'join us or perish in a lake of fire and blood', during bizarre scenes in which her eyes rolled back into her head, revealing nothing but emptiness.

Labour TD Burton, ageless, had been spotted acting erratically earlier in the session, as TDs made their case for the formation of a new government ahead of what proved to be fruitless attempts to elect a new Taoiseach.

The Labour leader was said to have been 'twitching and grimacing' while clutching a pencil in her right hand, which she was using to scrape macabre sketches into a little A5 jotter that she wasn't even looking at.

As the newly appointed Ceann Comharile Seán Ó Fearghail was addressing the chamber, Burton 'rose on one foot', pointed an upside-down hand at the assembled TDs, and chanted 'join us' for five minutes before collapsing to the ceiling.

'This is just a pitiful attempt by a depleted Labour party to maintain a foothold in the new government,' said one political and paranormal expert we spoke to. 'Burton has clearly formed a coalition with some form of malevolent spirit or djinn, and is attempting to get as many independent TDs and maybe even the Social Democrats to join her. It didn't work for Fianna Fáil in 2007, and it won't work here.'

Dáil admits they're not quite sure what the fuck the story is right now

Recently elected TDs have gone on record and admitted that when it comes to the matter of what exactly is happening right now, they aren't really all that sure.

February's General Election saw no party or coalition garner enough support to form a government, and there followed a Dáil vote to elect a Taoiseach in which no leader was elected. Enda Kenny stood down as Taoiseach, before re-appointing himself as a 'caretaker Taoiseach'.

Although most TDs are fairly sure they still have a job, they have agreed to stand up with the rest of the country and admit they're not sure 'just what the fuck the story is'.

'It's like when you were in school and the teacher wasn't in,' said one TD we spoke to. 'You're not sure if you have to stay, or if you can go home. As it is, we just come to Leinster House and sort of mill around the place until five o'clock, then tip on home.'

If you have an understanding of what the current situation is with the government of Ireland, WWN urges you to email your TD and bring him or her up to speed.

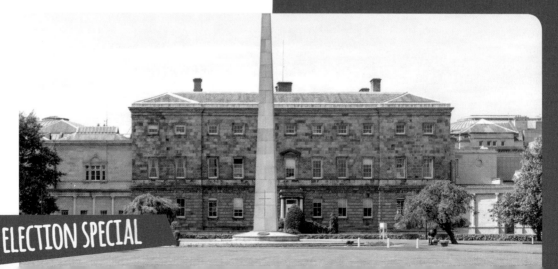

ELECTION SPECIAL

'How about you cunts get back to running the country!' yells nation

Following yet another failed attempt to form a government, an exhausted nation collectively broke its silence this evening after months of biting its lip.

In unison, over 4.5 million people yelled at the top of their voices in the general direction of Dublin city.

'How about you shower of cunts just get back to running the country' were the words heard echoing around the homeless-ridden Dublin city streets. 'We don't care who said what, or what points you didn't agree on – just get back to work and do your fucking jobs or we'll throw your sorry asses out of Leinster House.'

Unable to control itself any longer, the nation then complained about the lack of political choice in Ireland, pointing out that the majority of the people they're paying to run the country couldn't run a bath.

'We've got a delusional former Taoiseach, an ex-IRA commander and Mr Fucking Burns to pick from,' the nation went on. 'How about we sack all of them and start afresh? Maybe hire professional people who can actually take charge of finance, take charge of health, take charge of the country and ban school teachers with large egos from ever running for office again.'

With that said, the nation slowly calmed down and made itself a nice cup of tea, happy in the knowledge that it had said its piece – not that anyone was listening in the first place.

Mummified remains of election count staff found after nineteenth count

An investigation is under way after the bodies of thirty-nine counting staff were found mummified at their desks in a midlands election centre, some still clutching ballot papers.

It is believed that the dead may have been there since the weekend, and a tally board suggests they were on their nineteenth count.

Although the majority of Dáil seats have been filled following Friday's General Election, counting is continuing in some parts of the country, with transfers and unmet quotas delaying the election process.

These counting centres have been told to make sure staff are rested, fed and given plenty to drink to prevent a repeat of the tragic situation.

'It's like they were mid-count and just ... stopped living,' said the state pathologist who attended the grim scene. 'It's as if the process of being forced to do re-count after re-count just sucked the life out of them. From what we can gather, two of the three seats in the constituency had been filled, and there was a battle for the last seat between two independent candidates, separated by only five votes. In the end, it looks like these people just gave up and died.'

Following the removal of the bodies, a complete re-count of the ballot will commence later today.

ELECTION SPECIAL

Fine Gael changes Facebook status to 'in a relationship'

In what many social media experts are calling a 'premature' and 'cringe-inducing' move, Fine Gael have taken to its official Facebook page to confirm it is 'in a relationship', WWN can reveal.

Having sent an offer of cohabitation in Leinster House to Fianna Fáil, Fine Gael has already shared the good news that they have found that special someone to share power with.

'I don't know what they think this is, but it's way, way too early to put a label on it,' one Fianna Fáil TD told WWN, highlighting the fact that Fine Gael might have jumped the gun in going public with their affection and have now left themselves open to accusations of being 'way too keen'.

It is believed that after brief negotiations last night, Fine Gael leader and acting Taoiseach Enda Kenny felt confident that Micheál Martin was 'picking up what I was putting down'.

'Well Enda was calling Micheál a prick tease the other day, but he's happy they're shacked up now. He credits his trademark "let's ruin the country together" look as what swayed Fianna Fáil,' a spokesperson for Fine Gael explained to WWN.

Social media users have been quick to criticise Kenny, as screenshots of similar chat-up lines sent to Joan Burton in 2011 have surfaced online.

Fianna Fáil's relationship status still reads 'it's complicated' at the time of publication. More as we get it.

RTÉ hires more translators following Healy-Rae double victory

After being forced to admit that the Healy-Rae brothers are two of the most popular politicians in Ireland following a barnstorming performance in last Friday's General Election, officials at RTÉ have advertised three new job positions for anyone who can translate Kerry into English.

The successful applicant will be required to quickly and efficiently translate anything that either Michael Healy-Rae or his brother Danny Healy-Rae say during news broadcasts and live events, so that news staff will be able to converse with them.

Michael Healy-Rae was returned to Dáil Éireann after receiving more than 20,000 first preference votes; more than 7,000 over the quota and by far the most of any individual candidate across Ireland. He was followed by his brother Danny, making them the first brothers to be elected on the same day in the same constituency.

Begrudgingly admitting that their hard work in the Kerry community had pushed the Healy-Raes into the ranks of the best politicians in Ireland, RTÉ officials congratulated the pair and added that they hoped to be talking to them once a suitable translating service was in place.

'You have to hand it to them, they look after their people so their people looked after them,' said an RTÉ representative.

'We always thought they were just a pair of gombeen bullshit artists, but you don't get 20,000 votes without being a very shrewd, intelligent political force. So all we need now is someone who can translate what they're saying for Bryan Dobson on the Six One News, and we're set.'

RTÉ went on to state that the translator posts would be JobBridge positions, naturally.

LOCAL NEWS

'DO NOT LEAVE COMMENTS — ANYTHING YOU SAY MAY BE LIBELLOUS AND USED AGAINST YOU IN A COURT OF LAW.'

Waterford family describe heartbreak after learning teenage son has notions

One brave Waterford family has made the decision to talk publicly about the fact that their teenage son has notions, in a bid to help other families coping with the same situation.

Sharon and Keith O'Reilly posted an open letter on their Facebook pages to describe the heartbreak they felt after learning that their 18-year-old son Adam's battle with ideas above his station had worsened into full-blown notions.

It is believed that Adam contracted notions during the first term of an arts degree in UCD, and has

suffered symptoms such as cooking his own meals when he gets home at the weekend, and wearing clothes from a shop other than Penneys.

The tragic teenager no longer socialises with the people he went to secondary school with, and is believed to have a girlfriend in Dublin who is not Irish.

The O'Reilly family post on Facebook describing the difficulties of living with a notion-riddled teenager has been shared thousands of times.

'Sometimes he'll wake up on a Sunday morning, throw on a pair of tracksuit bottoms and sit watching *Pawn Stars*, and it's like the old Adam is back again,' wrote Sharon,

described online as 'Ireland's bravest woman'.

'Other times he'll come with me when I'm doing a shop to send back up to Dublin with him, and he'll insist on buying organic produce and soya milk. That's the thing with notions; it strips away everything you loved about the person, and just leaves a prick in its place.'

Since the open letter was posted on Facebook, the O'Reillys received the devastating news that Adam had just been cast in a UCD drama society production of *Glengarry Glen Ross*, a sure sign that his notions have escalated to stage 3, also known as uppityness.

Carlow man uses tattoo to display proud Maori heritage

One man is to commemorate his hitherto-unheard-of Maori heritage in a fearsome full-sleeve tribal tattoo, guaranteed to strike fear into the hearts of rival tribes surrounding his native town of Carlow.

Colm McCahill, 27, opted to honour his Maori ancestors with the hugely personal €789 pattern, which he conveniently found while flicking through a book of laminated designs in his local tattoo parlour.

Tribal tattoos, the mark of a warrior in many cultures, have been popular among white middle-aged men in Western Europe for many decades, and represent the struggles these men go through

from day to day, such as not being as cool as they'd like, and trying to look like a hard bastard on a 24/7 basis.

Although not much is known about the tribe of New Zealand warriors in central Carlow, McCahill's dedication to etching their markings on his body for life suggests that the community is both strong and proud.

'Check it out – it's like what The Rock has,' said McCahill, a plumber.

'Big swirls and then sharp bits and a face on my shoulder, like the sun. Most Maori warrior lads have

them, as well as all these lads that I go drinking with at the weekend. It was either get this or get like skulls and trees and shit like that all down my arm. I didn't really care to be honest, I just wanted something cool-looking for when I'm strolling round town with my top off in the summer.'

While communing with the spirits of ancient Maori tribal leaders, WWN discovered that they believe McCahill to be 'a bit of a sap'.

Croke Park residents warn Pope to not even think about it

Following hints that Pope Francis may be planning a visit to Ireland as early as 2018, members of the Croke Park Residents Association (CPRA) have come forward and told tour organisers that they know what they're thinking, and to not even attempt it.

Rumours about the pontiff's plans to come to Ireland emerged during his historic visit to the United States, when he confided to aides and archbishops that an Irish trip was 'not out of the question'.

This immediately sparked concerns of a repeat of the infamous Garth Brooks debacle, in which the country singer sold out five consecutive nights at the stadium, sparking a massive backlash from the CPRA that led to the gigs being cancelled.

The Year in Stats

2016 only had 11 months after the government scrapped May due to budget cuts.

It is feared that the mistakes of the past would be forgotten in the haste to make the Pope's visit as lucrative as possible, something the CPRA want to nip in the bud straight away.

'The Pope is more than welcome to come to Ireland, but we're not going

to have a million Catholics pissing on our lawns for a fortnight,' said one Croke Park resident, who likes Pope Francis but doesn't want him on her doorstep.

'A million people went to see Pope John Paul when he came here, and Croke Park holds eighty thousand or thereabouts, so there'd have to be two weeks of gigs to meet demand. Jog on, Francie – it's not happening.'

The GAA has yet to rule out inviting Pope Francis to Croke Park, and has released a statement extolling the economic benefits such an event could have for the community as well as their own pockets.

BREAKING NEWS

Dozens injured after pop-up restaurant suddenly appears on the M50

The reckless appearance of a restaurant specialising in organic, free-range, barbecue cooking in the middle lane of the M50 has been blamed for a multi-vehicle incident which led to hours of delays and dozens of injured motorists, it has been revealed.

Mulligans Snack Box, the latest pop-up restaurant to appear in the Dublin area, arrived unexpectedly after the N3 exit on the southbound lane of the M50 during morning rush hour, causing a multiple-vehicle collision as motorists tried in vain to avoid

hitting the structure which seemed to appear out of thin air.

'I was on my way to work as usual, minding my own business, and the next thing this restaurant just pops up out of nowhere,' said one lorry driver, who escaped with minor cuts and bruises.

'One minute the road was clear, then BAM!... there's a fuckin' chip shop or something in front of me. Last thing I remember is driving along listening to the radio, then having to swerve hard to avoid this lad with a beard handing out samples of pulled pork.'

The proprietors of Mulligans Snack Box, hashtag MSB, apologised for their choice of location for their pop-up restaurant, but insisted that food lovers in Dublin enjoy the spontaneity and feeling of exclusivity that comes with a temporary restaurant, before going on to offer anyone injured in the incident 50 per cent off any meat combo plate.

Gardaí attending the scene agreed to drop all charges against the restaurateurs after they were provided with brisket sandwiches.

Post-Paddy's Day clean-up to cost €14.5 billion

The total cost of the post-Paddy's Day clean-up has already reached €14.5 billion, the highest on record in the post-boom years, WWN can reveal.

As the public begins collecting their relatives and friends from the busy city streets on which they drunkenly fell asleep last night, local authorities are counting the cost of yet another large scale piss-up.

The Dublin Wheelbarrow Scheme, similar to the Dublin Bike Scheme, allows people free rental of wheelbarrows in order to transport their friends and family home, and is believed to cost the taxpayer several million euros.

'We've had the usual emergency spend on replacement livers – we have to dip into the black market for those on Paddy's Day, and they kill you with the price mark-up, they really do,' explained the resident surgeon at St Vincent's Hospital, Gregory Shanley.

Special pumps are hard at work on the country's waterways, clearing out the excess vomit that has found its way into the system, although it is believed this year's volume was no greater than in previous years.

A lot of post-Paddy's Day clean-up funds will have to be diverted to hospitals to treat several hundred men and women for exhaustion.

'Many people spend the day picking fights, and it really takes it out of them, God love them. They're absolutely pooped by the time the day is done,' explained Dr Abdul Abdhi, as he treated patients at Beaumont Hospital.

Inspirational Quote of the Year

'Yesterday is history, tomorrow a mystery and today is a gift. That's why we call it the present. I didn't pay attention in English class, but I'm sure that's why we call it the present.'

Local man reckons he could fight off ten, maybe twelve terrorists

The terrorist attacks in Paris and Nice have served to reassure one Dublin man that when it comes to fighting off jihadists in a kill or be killed situation, he could easily take up to twelve of them out of it.

Mark Brennan, 34, is confident that he could draw on nearly three decades of action movie experience to neutralise any situation in which he or his loved ones were threatened in an active shooter environment.

Having surveyed the carnage in Paris on Sky News, Brennan formulated a scenario in his head, in which he was in attendance at a location overrun by terrorists.

In this instance, the overweight and quite unfit Brennan easily disarmed the attacking mob using his imaginary black belt in imaginary fighting, winning the praise and adoration of everyone in attendance.

'I'd use the same techniques that I would have used if I was on board one of the planes that crashed into the twin towers,' said Brennan, staring out the window of the office he works in.

'The terrorist lads would be all ALLAH AKBAR, then I'd jump out and PAH PAH PAH ,WHACK! Problem solved. Maybe I'd get shot once, like in the shoulder. Just a flesh wound, nothing that would slow me down in any way.'

Brennan is also certain that he would be able to defuse any explosive device worn by extremists, providing it consisted of a large digital display and a choice between a red wire and a blue wire.

24 people shot dead in Dublin as Easter Rising re-enactment gets out of hand

Emergency services have closed central Dublin this afternoon after a band of Easter Rising re-enactment volunteers gunned down dozens of innocent people, leaving twenty-four dead and many more injured.

What began as a re-enactment of the 1916 rebellion, turned out to be Ireland's first mass shooting on the hundredth anniversary of the Easter Rising.

'They opened up on Temple Bar first,' an eyewitness told WWN. 'Everyone thought it was a joke, but the sound of bullets hitting bodies soon delivered the unwanted conclusion. They targeted British stag parties, but quite a few Irish people were hit too, which is a fairly accurate re-enactment when you think about it.'

It is understood that the group of part-time actors, who were dressed in rebel costume and carrying live weaponry, began shooting at 10:35 a.m., before unsuccessfully trying to make their way to the GPO in an attempt to replicate the rebel rising of one hundred years ago.

'On one hand, the re-enactment went very well indeed, but on the other, the unfortunate death of all those innocent people was probably unnecessary,' organiser Tom Partridge told WWN. 'I really don't know what happened – they just seemed to get carried away with the whole thing. I knew it was a risky idea to use live ammunition in the rifles. My bad.'

Gardaí have since locked down the city centre, as several re-enactment actors are still at large and defending a position at Moore Street.

Fucking loser likes his steak well done

A complete fucking loser ordered a fillet steak 'well done' in a County Waterford restaurant this evening, despite it being frowned upon by just about everyone who knows better.

Conor Moylan, who obviously doesn't get out much, requested the eight ounce lump of meat whilst dining with work friends, much to their utter embarrassment.

'I knew Conor was a bit of a bog warrior, but I didn't know he was this backward,' work colleague Dermot Tobin explained. 'He'll be digesting that until Christmas.'

'To make it worse, when the waiter asked if he wanted garlic butter or pepper sauce, he replied 'neither', and asked for ketchup instead,' added Tobin, who ordered his own steak 'bleu' in a bid to show everyone how different he is.

Unaware of his of own ignorance, Moylan also requested a 'pint of Ribena Orange' to accompany the meal, stating that he never could get used to 'that wine shite'.

'It all tastes the same to me,' he gloated, as if making some unique and humorous observation. 'Don't get me started on those fancy pansy beers either. The country is lost up its own hole lately. They'll be installing sparkling water taps in their sinks next.'

Surprisingly, Moylan went on to order the 'cheese board' for dessert, like it was nobody's business.

The Year in Stats

Irish people are 12% less sexy than last year, according to latest figures.

Gardaí finally taken off water meter duty to tackle crime

Members of An Garda Síochána were welcomed back this week after finally being taken off water meter duty in a bid to tackle actual crime.

Following their return, thousands of Gardaí were immediately deployed to Dublin city to help with ongoing searches relating to the Kinahan crime feud, which has resulted in several high-profile gangland deaths over the last six months.

'We've had to ease our boys back into it slowly, as they've been away for a few years and are a bit rusty,' Garda Commissioner Nóirín O'Sullivan told WWN, before going on to explain why Irish Water meter installers were present at many of the raids. 'We've had to hire a few water meter installers to help with the transition. They just kind of tag along with their red barriers for support and are handy when securing a premises that is being searched, since there is a court order banning the general public from entering their barrier space.'

So far this week, dozens of search warrants were issued by Gardaí investigating criminal activities in the city, which had a boom of their own during the recession, caused by depleted Garda numbers and a lack of financial resources.

'It's great that we can still have the chat and cup of tea with the water meter lads,' one Garda said. 'Now we can start dealing with real criminals, instead of doing jobs for the ones running the country.'

Strawberry picking slave labour: Wexford children speak out

The unforgiving Irish sun beat down on the N11 on Sunday afternoon. The scene before us was one familiar to all users of the famed connective tarmacked tissue between Dublin, Wicklow and Wexford – the hard shoulder was lined with workers, keen to earn a little extra cash on the weekends.

They'll sell forty-seven tonnes of strawberries every hour. Dubliners holidaying in Wexford have no qualms about being addicted to the red stuff. Native Wexicans are the same.

The number of workers will increase at the start of the summer when streams of children finish school. This is their story.

'I've been picking for eighty-nine hours straight,' one teen told us, admitting it had been so long since she'd last been to school that she

wasn't confident counting to eighty-nine any more.

Strawberries are the lifeblood of County Wexford, and the industry around the berry brings jobs to over seven million people every year. But with demand for the fruit increasing, strawberry barons are turning to less than legal means to procure what Wexicans call 'red gold'.

'I've been picking red gold ever since I can remember,' shared Ella, whose memory, to judge from her youthful face, can only stretch back as far as eighteen months at most because she is a toddler.

The younger the better is the word on the strawberry-planted ground. Children's small hands are perfect for picking strawberries, and toddler's tears hydrate the fruit, prolonging its shelf life.

For every teen who speaks out and runs from the awful work conditions, they leave behind a child barely able to speak at all. And that's

just how the strawberry barons like it. 'A bruised strawberry is money lost to me, and I can't have that. Teenagers these days have coarse, adult calluses on their hands, they're clumsy to boot, it disgusts me,' shared feared strawberry baron Gerard Conning, explaining why he now employs only children under the age of five on his farm.

'Toddlers are great. Plus they have no real concept of money so I can get away with paying them ten cents an hour. They think it's great because it jingles in their little Dora the Explorer purses. Stupid babies.'

Conning showed no remorse for his actions, and what shocked us most of all was that once we had sampled the strawberries on offer at the farm, we didn't care either. They tasted so juicy, so refreshing, we instantly came to the conclusion that Conning wasn't a bastard at all, but a sound and solid businessman who gave the world amazing strawberries.

BUSINESS

Car insurers now giving away free Vaseline with every policy

Car insurance providers are attempting to take the sting out of the recent hikes in the cost of motor insurance by throwing in free gifts such as tubs of Vaseline, Sudocrem and Bepanthen with every policy.

Many motorists are facing hikes in the region of 40 per cent in the cost of their car insurance with brokers stating that the increases are necessary because they realised that they wanted more money.

Even drivers with flawless on-the-road histories and decades of no-claims bonuses are looking at an increase of several hundred euro on their premiums, prompting insurance brokers across the country to give away free ointments and balms to help 'soothe the pain of getting f****d in the ass'.

'Several motorists will find that their policy is now well over €1,000 and for that we offer a very special gift: one of those rubber rings that you get after rectal surgery,' said Ian Massey, spokesperson for the Car Insurance Cartel Of Ireland.

'So after we kick your hole with our hiked costs, at least you have something to help nurse your hole back to full health. Hey, we didn't want to turn around out of nowhere and hike prices way the fuck up ... but then we realised that there's nothing you can do about it, so we went ahead and did it.'

Four thousand students who failed maths to be welcomed into banking sector

Although this morning's Leaving Cert results indicating that up to four thousand students failed to receive a passing grade in mathematics may have disappointed many, there was optimism on the horizon as the banking sector swooped in and offered high-ranking positions to all.

Almost 55,000 students received their results this morning, with a stark warning about the state of maths tuition in Ireland lurking in the jump from 5.8 per cent to 9 per cent in the failure rate of ordinary level maths students.

Not having a pass in maths may have put paid to the third-level dreams of many students who had applied for courses in which a pass in mathematics is mandatory, but there was joy as the Financial Regulator of Ireland issued a statement declaring that the ability to understand mathematics was not required when working in the banking sector.

'You want a job, you've got one,' said a spokesperson for the Central Bank. 'Fuck it, if you can do basic arithmetic, you're halfway there. You don't have to worry too much about always getting everything correct, or indeed being responsible for the calamity that bad book-keeping and rash mathematical assumptions might cause. As long as you've got the right type of hard-nosed, brass-balled attitude to working in banking, there's a job waiting for you.'

Although maths may not be all that necessary when working in banking, the sector warned that a second language, such as German, could prove very handy in years to come.

Financial pearls of wisdom from Economics Correspondent Freddy Nobbs

When saving for that first mortgage be sure to rob your local newsagents right before they close as that's when there will be the most money in the till.

Lidl to hire six hundred people as part of ambitious 'second till' plans

Supermarket giant Lidl has announced six hundred new jobs in Ireland as part of wildly ambitious plans to have a second till open in all their stores by 2020.

'When we started out it was never our plan to have a second till,' head of Lidl's Strategic Second Till Planning Squad (LSSTPS) Bryan Colgan explained to WWN. 'The lad who did the interiors of all our shops had actually suffered a bang on his head and was seeing double at the time of kitting out the shops. We specifically said one till only,' Colgan added.

It is believed Lidl will become the first-ever supermarket chain to install a second till on a permanent basis. New staff will be trained up by Lidl in the coming months, and painstaking attention to detail will be demanded from them.

'The training will be big on "Sit at second till. Serve customers at second till. Keep second till open at all times." We've never been more serious about second tills in our lives. We're surprised no other supermarket has ever thought about doing this before, to be honest,' Colgan conceded.

Customers have warmly welcomed the move but some people remain unconvinced and even worried at the announcement.

'This is madness, it's too ambitious, it's the shopping equivalent of trying to fly to Mars in a cardboard box. Lidl stores operate like a delicate ballet of long queues and only open tills when people start pulling their hair out. Without this structure in place chaos will reign,' consumer affairs expert Colm Glennon explained to WWN.

BUSINESS

Facebook urges users not to be so fucking gullible

Pinching the bridge of his nose, Facebook CEO Mark Zuckerberg took to the podium at a press conference today and appealed to users of his popular social media network to stop being so God damn gullible when it comes to sharing bullshit about changes in Facebook policy.

The press conference was called after hundreds of thousands of idiots fell for yet another copy and paste chain letter which claimed Facebook was about to introduce a premium service which would require a monthly subscription.

The chain letter went on to state that anyone who didn't sign up to this service would have all their photos sold to evil corporations who would use the images in adverts for haemorrhoid cream, Fianna Fáil posters and hardcore pornography.

'And of course, the only way to prevent this is to post a status on Facebook saying that you don't agree to these terms,' said Zuckerberg, who has just about had it with this shit.

'Do you people even read this crap before you copy and paste it? Or does it just punch your moron button hard enough to get a reaction? Honestly, do you think our legal team combs through the profiles of the billion or so Facebook users, looking to see did they post some garbage about whether or not you consent to the terms of some made-up bullshit? I despair sometimes, I really fucking do.'

Zuckerberg went on to state that if he ever did decide to change the privacy policies of Facebook, 'you people would never even know it had happened', before an aide stepped up and took the mic away.

EXCLUSIVE

Dublin Bus to trial new 'Arrive on Time' service

Dublin Bus confirmed the launch of a new service they call 'Arrive on Time' at a glitzy press event on O'Connell Street earlier today.

The bus operators invited five hundred of their most valued daily commuters to the launch, but there was considerable confusion as the customers struggled to comprehend what the new service involved.

'What? I don't understand. I presume I just arrive at my stop a good forty minutes before the bus is due to be late, just in case, right?' one panicked commuter shouted from the crowd.

The majority of the five hundred commuters in attendance were bang on time for the press event as they chose to walk from home or cycle in.

'It's like the normal bus service, only when it says it'll be due in five minutes, it will actually arrive in five minutes instead of disappearing altogether,' a Dublin Bus official explained to a crowd full of blank stares.

Dublin Bus had planned to demonstrate the service on O'Connell Street for their commuters by asking them to wait for one of their new on-time buses. However, due to Luas works, the bus was delayed by some fourteen hours.

'I don't like change like this,' one regular commuter explained to WWN. 'Can't we just keep it the old way? It's nice to know you can just leave the house at 6.30 in the morning and catch a bus which gets you in about an hour late for work at 10 a.m.'

The Arrive on Time service is expected to be rolled out on one route on a trial basis some time in 2019.

Financial pearls of wisdom from Economics Correspondent Freddy Nobbs

Although they look very realistic, chocolate coins are not legal tender.

Irish people under the impression government would spend Apple's €13bn on them

In yet another example of how Irish people are the most naive species in the known universe, a new poll shows that almost the entire population is under the impression that the government would spend the €13bn Apple tax windfall on things like public services.

'I think it's a great boost for the country ... just think what €13 billion could do for the health service,' said one poor gobshite, who has forgotten how Irish politics works.

'Think of what this money will mean to future generations,' added another simpleton, oblivious to the fact that not one citizen in the country has even the slightest hope of seeing a cent of the money.

The survey was taken in the wake of an EU ruling that declared that Apple availed of illegal state aid, resulting in billions of lower-than-fair taxes over the years.

The tech giant was ordered to cough up €13 billion in arrears, which led to public outrage in Ireland when the government insisted that they would appeal the decision and let Apple keep the money.

Uproar across the country revolved around people yelling about how Ireland could use that cash to 'reinstate services lost through years of austerity', proving conclusively that nobody has paid much attention to how Irish politicians work.

'Lads ... you do know that €13 billion would just go straight into paying off the EU, don't you?' said a bewildered Michael Noonan earlier today. 'It would never touch the ground here. We'd never see it. We wouldn't have a pallet of cash sitting in a storage place like in *Breaking Bad*. Come on now. It'd come off the bailout money, and neither me nor anyone else would would be able to do anything about it. Believe me, I'd love to have an extra €13 billion of free money all of a sudden. It'd be pay rises all round in Leinster House.'

Meanwhile, Apple has announced the creation of three new jobs in Ireland, cementing the belief that we should just give them their money back 'because they're sound'.

BUSINESS

WWN guide to smiling politely when an American says 'I'm Irish'

It may rank as one of the most infuriating experiences for an Irish person, but due to the high levels of foreign direct investment the nation enjoys from America, you must continue to smile politely when a US citizen informs you that they are 'Irish' or face the possible ruin of our entire economy.

Such politeness is proving harder and harder to muster, so WWN's guide to nodding and smiling in an effort to hide your displeasure could not come at a better time.

'My granny was from, I think it's pronounced "Conny-mary"'

Don't take the bait. That anger which has covered your every fibre like a warm, violent blanket is not to be trusted. When faced with an American harmlessly sharing with you their heritage you must reject your anger or take responsibility for the catastrophic fallout.

Do not correct their ear-shattering mispronunciation of Connemara – instead think of the first time you ever saw a breast on TV, or in the cinema ... yes, that's it, Kate Winslet's boobs in *Titanic*. Let the anger subside.

'It's my first time here, going to visit my second cousins sixteen times removed. Say, you couldn't point me in the direction of a pot of gold, could ya? Ha ha!'

Put down the knife. No, stop it. Christ, that's a lot of blood. Jesus, yer man isn't looking too good now. Clean your fingerprints off the knife and run. Don't look back. Actually, wait, take his wallet, make it look like a mugging. Keep the head down, say nothing. This will all blow over in a few days.

'We're so happy to finally be here to experience our heritage. You must be so proud of all your country has achieved here and abroad. The Irish people have given so much to the world.'

Okay, first off, shut the fuck up, condescending to us, you walking advertisement for Weight Watchers – that's what you shouldn't say, obviously. Remember, calm, deep breaths. In a few short months from now there won't even be an America anymore, because of Donald Trump.

'My granddad was from Cork, but I won't bore you with that bullshit. Anyway would you happen to know if the GPO is up this way? Thanks.'

Check. Out. This. Prick. Don't let that anger in, though – smile, smile, that's it, and now give them directions to Tallaght, still smiling. That American is going to get so lost it's not even funny. Good job.

Most Downloaded Apps in Ireland in 2016

1. Dublin Gangland Hit Tracker

2. Is Denis O'Brien Suing Me Right Now?

3. What Are the 1916 Leaders' Names Again?

4. Culchie Translator

5. Where's My Phone?

Student five months into philosophy course disappears up own hole

A first-year philosophy student currently attending UCD has disappeared up his own hole after becoming well versed in the musings of Barthes, Plato and Camus.

'Initially Mark was mostly visible to the naked eye,' explained long-time friend of Mark Brearton, Cathal Cowan. 'But I saw it happening and

The Year in Stats

100% of the nation is unable to name all 32 counties on their first attempt.

sadly I did nothing as he ever so slowly disappeared up his own hole.'

Brearton, a previously engaging and well-meaning 18-year-old, shifted conversational style upon first coming into contact with the ideas of existentialism and reason – from that of an unpretentious and keen learner to a style more befitting someone who purely enjoyed the sound of his own voice.

'He said to me, "Once you've appraised Barthes's work, you're sort of always going to send yourself down this deconstructionist path, well look, this isn't evident to you, but you should open yourself up to art not through the prism of the artist,"

and that was the last time I saw him,' another friend of Brearton's, Vicky Kearns, told WWN.

'I would have put up missing posters, or called his folks to see if they'd seen him, but it was pretty obvious he had disappeared up his own hole,' Kearns added.

Gardaí have been strongly critical of UCD philosophy lecturers as Brearton is the thirty-ninth student to go missing up his own hole, never to be seen again.

'Not only will he likely never be found, he also leaves a trail of parties and social outings ruined by his shite talk,' confirmed Garda Gerry Nolan, head of the Garda Anti-Own-Hole Unit.

Joy as man who said 'Boom' after every sentence finally explodes

'Just scored two tickets to the All-Ireland final, boom!' Those were the last words of Aidan Meehan before he exploded all over the inside of his office cubicle, according to co-workers who witnessed the grim scene.

Staff at McKillan & Byrne accountants were said to be overjoyed at Meehan exploding, although many admitted that they wished it had happened outside office hours.

Meehan, 25, had become a hated figure in the busy Dublin

office due to his habit of ending self-congratulatory statements with the word 'boom', sometimes changed to 'boomage' or 'boomzo'.

The Raheny native would use the word at the end of statements in which he detailed his skill at dealing with wealthy clients, his sexual triumphs at the weekend, and instances where he managed to get a scrumpled-up ball of paper into the bin across from his desk with one overhead throw.

The habit irritated his co-workers to such an extent that many of them wanted to punch Meehan 'right in his stupid fucking face', although calmer heads prevailed and the decision was made to just let him keep saying it until he eventually exploded.

'I must say, his last boom was his best one,' chuckled co-worker Janet Kilbride, 36. 'It's great to know that we never have to hear him tell us how he "played a blinder at five-a-side last night, boom", or have to return a fist-bump and hear him make an exploding noise.'

Exploding after saying 'boom' at the end of a sentence claims more lives every year than anything else. As such, people are advised to just stop doing it, immediately.

Man trapped in Budweiser warehouse resorts to drinking his own urine

A Dublin man has told reporters of his harrowing experience after becoming trapped for three days in a Budweiser storage depot, during which time he was forced to drink his own urine to stay alive.

Malcolm McArdle, 35, was working at the beer warehouse on Friday evening when he accidentally got locked in by co-workers after returning to grab his phone from the cab of his forklift.

Thinking that McArdle had left already, staff at the depot closed the shutters and went home for the weekend, leaving the Dublin native trapped in the inner part of the store.

With his phone battery dead and surrounded only by crates of Budweiser beer, McArdle had no choice but to wait for nearly three days to be freed with nothing to eat and absolutely nothing that he could drink.

'The thirst really started to kick in on Saturday,' said McArdle, recovering at his home following his ordeal. 'I tried to lick condensation off the walls, but that didn't work. In the end, I had to open a can of Budweiser, pour it all out, fill the empty can with my own piss and drink that. I'm not ashamed: I did what I had to do to survive.'

Workers arrived at the warehouse to clock in on Monday morning and discovered the emaciated McArdle, who was immediately rushed to hospital suffering from severe dehydration. Checks are being put in place to make sure an incident like this never happens again.

Splinter farmer group declares itself the 'Real IFA'

A group of dissident farmers calling itself the Real IFA has issued a statement in which it claims it will bring 'order and stability to Irish farming' by any means necessary.

It is believed the group broke away from the Irish Farmers' Association following controversy about the resignation of General Secretary Pat Smith, after revelations that his annual salary was in excess of €400,000 per annum.

Disgusted at being part of an organisation in which grassroots members earn less than one fifteenth of that figure, several hundred rogue farmers created the 'Real IFA', which they claim will act in the best interests of Irish farmers

and continue the campaign against 'any aul nonsense'.

Speaking from an undisclosed location, a spokesperson for the agricultural group made stark warnings about upcoming disruption and events that the new splinter group would be involved in.

'Villages, towns, cities … Nowhere is safe from our tractors,' said the Real IFA spokesman, his face disguised by a smearing of what may or may not have been Nutella.

'For too long, the people of Ireland have had to deal with the IFA, which has grown soft and weak as the years have gone by. The Real IFA will strike fear into the hearts of governments and commuters, as we bring protests the likes of which have never been seen before to this land.'

Government analysts have declared that while the Real IFA is promoting itself as acting in the best interests of the people, the operation may just be a front for illegal activity such as milk laundering and black-market Ivomec dealing.

School having 'prom' instead of a debs would want to cop onto itself

A Waterford school, which has decided to hold an American style 'prom', has been told to cop onto itself, WWN has learned.

The sixth year class of St Brendan's College, together with their principal, agreed that a theme which sought to replicate the clichés of an American high-school prom was just what this year's debs ball needed.

'Christ, they've themes now for debs? Mine was held on the back of a trailer dragged along by a tractor and we didn't complain,' shared Martin Devlin, the concerned parent of a student at St Brendan's.

The official prom theme is said to be 'Shitfaced Under the Sea' and will require students to wear marine-inspired dresses and suits.

'Aren't debs and proms basically the same thing?' queried another parent who was questioning why the cost of the debs had gone up by €100 as a result of becoming a prom.

Some community commentators have suggested St Brendan's thinks it's better than everyone else.

'What's wrong with a good old-fashioned Irish debs? Skulling a naggin in the toilets and then getting sick isn't bad craic – you'd swear this St Brendan's crowd were ashamed of their culture. Sake,' remarked local busybody Elaine Hurley.

BEHIND THE HEADLINES

Early census information reveals 120 per cent of the nation is Catholic

With census enumerators in the midst of collecting census forms from the nation's households, one trend is emerging which suggests there's been little change from the last census, which was conducted in 2011.

Some 120 per cent of the nation has identified itself as Catholic, thanks in no small part to the diligent work of parents, who have insisted on listing their children as such on census forms in spite of objections from their offspring.

'We're right on track to match our 2011 total, which basically means we can keep being that seemingly benign yet overbearing influence in your life, whether you like it or not,' confirmed Fr Augustine Spring, spokesperson for the Catholic church in Ireland.

'However, we're not entirely happy as this new "No religion" religion is becoming more popular. We'll have a word with everyone's mam, and she'll easily have that shite snuffed out by the time we do this census thing again in five years,' Fr Spring confirmed.

The information gathered in the census will be used to help shape future governmental policy when it comes to matters such as education and public services, and so far the Central Statistics Office (CSO) are happy with what they see.

'We don't want specific results one way or another, but that residual Catholic guilt hangover just means we can essentially use the 2011 results without doing much extra work poring over the new ones,' CSO spokesman John Hingle explained.

The CSO also rejected all accusations that the Catholic church had tampered with the census results, stating that when it comes to tampering with the public's minds, the church has been putting in the groundwork over several centuries.

Phone box found in convicted drug dealer's prison cell

Officials at a Dublin prison are today investigating the smuggling of a 7 x 3-foot telephone box, after a routine sweep unveiled the fully functioning calling booth situated in the corner of a convicted drug dealer's cell.

Kevin Keane, a Dublin criminal who was sentenced to four years for the possession of five kilograms of heroin, refused to explain how the antique telephone box was smuggled into his cell and attached to the main prison landline.

'When we entered Mr Keane's cell, there were several inmates queueing to use the coin-operated phone box,' Mountjoy governor Brian Murphy recalled. 'Not only that, but we were told to "get to the back of the queue" by Keane, before he realised who we were. We found over €4,000 in change under his bed, and several hundred phone cards.'

Prison officers ordered all inmates to return to their cells while a forensic team investigated the find.

'We found traces of human faeces all around the box, which would suggest it was smuggled orally into the prison,' Governor Murphy added.

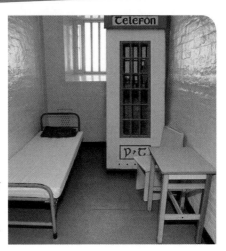

Sources have said the box may have been there for several months, giving inmates direct and unmonitored contact with the outside world.

Goths battle skateboard kids for control of Central Bank territory

In what is set to be one of the most bloodless battles the city of Dublin has ever known, two opposing armies of sullen teenagers are to clash this Saturday to see who gets to hang outside the front of the Central Bank: the Goth kids or the skateboarders.

Both factions have shared an uneasy truce for years, with the sullen-faced Emo and Goth kids taking up the right-hand side, and the baggy-trousered skateboarders doing little jumps off the disabled ramp on the left.

From the moment their parents drop them off in the morning until the moment their parents pick them up in the evenings, both groups loiter around the area, occasionally taking a break from laughing at nothing in particular to go sit on the kerb around the bank and French-kiss badly.

Although the territory has been shared for years, there has been tension recently, caused by one teenager bumping into another, and this has caused a war of words between the sides, which will be settled on Saturday.

'We are met at this chosen ground to settle for good and all who holds sway over the Central Bank: us Goths, or the skateboarding hordes defiling it,' said one teenager, probably called Jeremy with a double-barrelled surname.

'We have more of a right to be here because we're cooler; I have a tattoo, you know. My mam hit the roof but I don't care. I wrote a poem about it. And I'll write a poem about this Saturday too, when we stare those skateboard kids out of it until they fuck off once and for all.'

While right-minded citizens are going to do their best to avoid the Central Bank area on Saturday as usual, the square in Temple Bar is bracing itself for refugees from both camps.

Amazing new app raises your child until the age of 18

Parents are rejoicing at news of a brand new app released for both Android and iOS that claims to be able to keep your kids out of your hair until they're old enough to vote.

Dubbed 'Tabletmirror', the app replicates the functions of any tablet or smartphone that it gets downloaded to, allowing the user to do anything that they would normally do on a tablet.

By handing this to a child of any age, the youngster will be able to play games, browse the internet, watch videos on YouTube and chat with people all across the world.

Research has found that when a kid is using a tablet that has the Tabletmirror app on it, they will sit perfectly still and remain contented for as long as the wi-fi connection holds up. This will allow parents to have a moment for themselves to cook the dinner, make a phone call, or just sit in peace and quiet for a few years.

Further studies show that kids simply never get tired of this app as it adjusts to suit them as they grow up, meaning that they will sit there until they're old enough to buy cigarettes.

'Here we see a kid without Tabletmirror,' said a TM spokesperson, pointing to a screen showing a young child trying to get their parents' attention. 'And here we see a kid using Tabletmirror; you see they have no interest in interacting with anyone or anything. It's almost as if they haven't got parents to begin with.'

As well as being useful around the home, Tabletmirror is also suitable for car journeys, holidays and meals at restaurants.

Government plans to raise Ireland by 500 metres to avoid future flooding

The Irish government has announced a massive €456bn project to raise the island of Ireland by as much as 500 metres above sea level to avoid future flooding.

Taoiseach Enda Kenny proposed the elevation of the entire country at an emergency meeting held at Leinster House this morning, which was later passed by TDs in a comfortable majority vote.

The project, which is expected to be finished by December 2016, will see all twenty-six counties raised by almost half a kilometre using a ground-breaking new inflation system that will elevate the landmass to the desired height, before filling the five-hundred-metre void underneath with a new waterproof foundation.

'This procedure should guarantee the future safety of our citizens when it comes to global warming and the rise in sea-levels,' assured Taoiseach Enda Kenny. 'Obviously there will be a bit of a drop down to the six counties in the North, but we have a cable-car system to put in place there for the time being.'

The news comes after Minister of State with responsibility for the Office of Public Works reported that the cost of the clean-up after recent flooding would be more than €8 million and defended the cost of the €456bn project, stating it would pay off in the long run.

'It's just common sense,' the minister explained. 'It's either live in a submarine or a boat. I know which one I'd rather.'

Met Éireann instructs nation to stay indoors until next summer

Ireland is today experiencing its most severe level of weather warning as Met Éireann instructed the nation to stay indoors until next summer, which traditionally starts in July and lasts about five days.

Speaking to WWN, Met Éireann stressed that the fact that its staff had agonised over using the most severe weather warning available to them should make clear to the public just how awful the conditions are out there.

'It's fucking cat out there, isn't it? I'm going to get hate mail for fucking weeks now,' explained a concerned Barry Corless, chief meteorologist at Met Éireann.

Corless confirmed Met Éireann would take a few days, confident in the fact that the weather would stay 'fairly shite altogether', only picking up sometime in the middle of next year.

'I'd happily take the first half of the year, but then who is going to come up with the names for all those class storms?' Corless queried.

Others at Met Éireann confirmed they were taking no chances when it came to warning the public about the adverse conditions.

'We at Met Éireann have experienced two eras in weather reporting. There is BMFOIORTEN (Before man falling on ice on RTÉ News) and AMFOIORTEN (After man falling on ice on RTÉ News),' explained meteorologist Hannah Grehan.

'We knew we had to issue our "it's shit" weather warning, the most severe warning available to us, if only to save a number of people from injuring themselves in public. We've learned from man falling on ice,' Grehan added.

'Pure and utter shite': WWN reviews local school nativity play

When we received an invitation to a nativity play at St Bertie Ahern Primary School in Waterford city last Monday, everyone in WWN towers begged for the assignment as it was yet another chance to write about Christmas and, more importantly, a chance to get out of the office.

Pulling the short straw, I could hardly contain my excitement as my colleagues cursed my good luck. However, my celebrations were short-lived when I arrived at the school.

Entering the school gate, I was greeted by principal Gerard Hanley, a thin man in a tweed jacket with leather elbow patches, who ushered me upstairs to a room packed with anxious parents and children, all waiting for the teacher's cue to start.

'Okay everyone, this is Patrick Browne and he is a journalist for local newspaper *Waterford Whispers News*,' Mr Hanley explained. 'Patrick will be writing a review of today's performance so I want everyone to do their very best.'

'Be kind to them now,' he said, half-laughing for some reason. 'These kids have been rehearsing all week.'

I took Hanley's comments on board, but as a veteran journalist of twenty-seven years, I was here to do my job.

Following several half-hearted introductions to some teachers and parents, I sat myself at the front to get a good vantage point.

Introducing the play was 5-year-old Tommy Hutchinson, a brazen-looking child with blonde hair. Tommy's narration was excellent, but I couldn't help feeling

he was a little distracted by a ghastly middle-aged woman with an iPhone who kept waving at him – probably his mother. This inevitably ruined the child's performance for me, but I blame the parent for that and not Tommy.

Intro

Tommy managed to set the tone for the play: some angel appeared to a woman called Mary telling her she was blocked up with God's baby. Her husband seemed cool about it, but they had to head off on a broom together (which I was later told was a donkey) to a town called Bethlehem to fill out some paperwork. Basically, the story of Jesus' birth. And when I say basically, I mean that these kids were basically terrible actors.

Several group songs interrupted the play all the way through, and to be honest, I don't think it worked. The kids were out of tune and

some didn't even know the words. One kid didn't sing at all. It was a disaster. What bugged me more was the fact this was advertised as a 'play', not a musical.

Performances

I found the lead actors dreadful. I know St Bertie Ahern's is an all boys' school, but they could have borrowed a girl from neighbouring St Twink's to play Mary, because Timothy fucking Jones was absolutely brutal.

Not only did Timothy not even try to mimic a woman's voice, he couldn't fake labour pains if his life depended on it. Not even a look of shock when the angel Gabriel broke the good news. Nothing. He just stood there like a little dope with his freckly mouth open.

Mark Tracey portrayed Joseph very well. As in, he said nothing all the way through and looked largely vacant in the background. An easy role one might think, but very hard to pull off. So well done Mark.

Now, where do I start with the innkeeper, the three wise men and the shepherds? It's not good news I'm afraid. These children should all be told that under no circumstance should they set foot on a stage again … not even as stage hands.

The innkeeper messed up his lines, twice. One of the three wise men couldn't even pronounce frankincense, or 'fwankenstine' as he kept calling it, and the

shepherds looked more like Saudi Arabian oil dealers than astronomers. My advice to the teachers and parents would be to focus their children's attention on more academic subjects that don't require them to pretend they're someone else.

So, who's to blame?

After the play was over, many of the parents came up and asked me what I thought, so I told them the truth: 'pure and utter shite'.

Unfortunately, this did not go down well. Several parents began cursing at me in front of their own children, calling me horrific names I cannot repeat here: wanker, evil bastard, horrible prick. I told them it wasn't my fault that the casting was done so badly and that their kids were pathetic actors. I suggested hiring real kid actors for next year's show and dumping the musical numbers because they were so bad; something the class teacher didn't like hearing, of course, because she organised this whole fucking disaster.

I urged parents to attack the teacher instead, but my appeals fell on deaf ears and I had to leave quite quickly due to an angry Polish dad who was being held back by a group of teachers.

Summary

St Bertie Ahern's senior infants' nativity play was shite at best. The whole thing was a shambles from start to finish. The costumes looked like they were pulled out of a charity-shop skip. The audience were biased and there were too many people illegally filming the play on their phones. Like, enjoy the moment in real life, people!

What annoyed me most was how petty the children were when I tried to give them valuable feedback after the show, and how sensitive everyone was to my valid points. As the saying goes: if you can't take the heat, stay out of the kitchen.

Inspirational Quote of the Year

'Everything happens for a reason, even sharts.'

Nation to spend next four weeks getting 'last few bits and pieces'

Despite spending this past weekend shopping for the last few bits and pieces, the nation's consumers will spend every weekend between now and Christmas shopping for even more last few bits and pieces, and may also require a trip to the shops on Christmas Eve for 'the very last' few bits and pieces.

Bits and pieces, integral to the enjoyment of any Christmas activities, have been on sale since mid-August, the beginning of the festive shopping season.

Most savvy shoppers have spent the last few weekends in November stocking up on the most important bits and pieces, narrowing their 'bits and pieces' list down one bit and one piece at a time.

Having the bulk of their bits and pieces already bought, most consumers are looking forward to a restful December, free of traffic-congested trips to overcrowded supermarkets and shopping centres. The last weekend in November is the cut-off point for many, as they head to town centres to get the very last few bits and pieces they need to feed and clothe themselves for winter, as well as decorate their houses and buy presents for everyone.

However, studies suggest that even though people may feel they have everything they need, there are still a few stealth bits and pieces unaccounted for, necessitating further trips to the shops between now and 25 December.

'There is no such thing as a definitive bits and pieces list,' said Ian Jordan, consumer expert. 'It's like the horizon. You may think you've reached it, but it just keeps moving further away. So even though you think you're all done because you made the trip to the shops to get Christmas crackers, Worcestershire sauce and batteries for the Santa ornament that plays piano, rest assured you have still to go next weekend and get something for your kid's teacher, a new corkscrew, and maybe a plastic link for the toilet handle because it won't flush properly.'

Jordan went on to add that although the vast majority of these bits and pieces would still be available from the 26 December onwards, you need to get them by 24 December or your Christmas is ruined.

Dublin Airport evacuated after build up of Guinness farts

Hundreds of people were briefly evacuated from Terminal 2 in Dublin Airport this morning after a series of Guinness farts engulfed the departures lounge.

'It's Christmas and we've had a lot of people drinking the black stuff at the airport and things got out of hand,' said spokesperson for Dublin Airport Authority, Siobhan O'Donnell. 'The smell got so bad at one point that several staff members had to be treated for septic shock. Eventually we had to evacuate parts of the terminal around the bar area.'

Following today's incident, all passengers will be restricted to just fourteen pints of Guinness per person in a bid to reduce the release of toxins in the airport.

'This is the third time this year we've had to evacuate the airport due to the smell of Guinness farts,' Ms O'Donnell added. 'At least we've been able to keep it contained to the departures lounge – it has not reached arrivals, where our valuable tourists come through. With this fourteen-pint restriction, we should hopefully have all farts under control by this evening.'

Along with a code yellow Guinness fart warning, the airport has also issued a code red shart warning for all passengers who ingest the popular stout.

'Just don't trust your farts' a large warning sign read at the airport bar. 'We do not take any responsibility for soiled garments.'

Santa Claus arrested for drink flying in Dublin

Gardaí in Dublin have confirmed that they have arrested Santa Claus for flying while under the influence of alcohol after he attempted to take off from a residential rooftop in Swords.

Mr Claus, who was breathalysed at the scene, was found to have a blood alcohol concentration of 50.34, making him more than one hundred times over the legal limit.

'We stopped a large stocky man about to get into a sleigh at 5.30 p.m,' arresting Garda Diarmuid Casey told WWN. 'Mr Claus couldn't even speak or stand up straight so we arrested him on suspicion of flying a reindeer-propelled vehicle while under the influence of alcohol. Mr Claus agreed to give a breath sample, which immediately turned red, indicating he was over the limit.'

Gardaí transported the North Pole resident to Swords Garda station for further testing, which revealed the extent of his drinking.

'This is the highest reading we've ever had in this country, which is impressive considering it's Ireland,' confirmed Garda Casey.

In his defence, Mr Claus said he had been travelling all day and was going to be finished soon, adding that it wasn't his fault that so many alcoholic beverages were left out for him by children.

Due to his arrest, presents will not be delivered to the Americas.

WORLD NEWS

'LET'S MAKE AMERICA GREAT AGAIN!'

Capitalist extremists blow up 85 civilians in Syria, including 11 children

At least 85 civilians, including 11 children, have been killed by Western-led terrorists in air strikes near Manbij in north Syria.

Some eight families were obliterated by sophisticated missiles as they tried to flee their village after it was attacked in one of the single deadliest strikes on innocent civilians in the region.

Capitalist extremists were immediately held responsible for the attack by the Syrian Observatory for Human Rights.

'So far over 200 of my people, including 44 children and 20 women have been killed in Manbij by capitalist extremists since the start of June,' a local man, who now has a Syrian flag as his Twitter profile picture, told WWN. 'Just who are these insane people and why do they want to terrorise our rural village? Why aren't they being held responsible for their actions?'

On Monday, Facebook launched a Safety Check for people affected by the spate of bombings in Syria, while dozens of cartoonists and artists from across the world have created some fantastic images in solidarity with the victims of Manbij. The hashtag #ManbijAttack is now trending on Twitter with several high-profile celebrities posting pictures of themselves burning dollar bills in protest at the Western terrorists.

Sources on the ground in Syria believe the terrorists operate under the guise of political jargon and mostly hail from corrupt Western countries, like the prominently capitalist United States of America. It is understood the extremists are killing people remotely with sophisticated military hardware, attempting to free themselves from all responsibility for their actions.

In a worrying development, upcoming elections in the Western region, which have already been beset by allegations of voter fraud, have become a prime opportunity for mobilising extremists as the two leading candidates have preached a message of future aggression on foreign soil.

These capitalist fundamentalists have vowed to destroy anyone or anything that refuses to adhere to the word of their prophet, Dollar.

BRITISH NEWS

Muslims urged to stop dressing up like terrorists

Security forces in the UK are calling on people of the Islamic faith to rethink their dress code due to the alarming resemblance between Muslim and terrorist attire.

David Freeman, a high-level security expert for MI5, has urged British Muslims to dispense with their current attire of burkas and headscarves and to adopt more typically Western fashion choices.

'It is ridiculous that many Muslims choose to dress up like terrorists every day,' he stated in a brief interview on Sky News. 'Why would they be so stupid? Everyone knows what a terrorist looks like, so why mimic them?'

Sky News host Cath Hall also pointed out that 'that lot also wear turbans', adding weight to Freeman's helpful comments on the British Muslim community.

Following the tragic events in Paris and Beirut which saw the deaths of hundreds of innocent people, British security forces are on high alert over possible attacks by Islamic State members.

'You don't see Irish people walking around with balaclavas and camo jackets on, so why must you people?' Freeman said, in a direct challenge to Muslims and making reference to a time when all Irish people wore IRA uniforms. 'It's just common sense. Save those costumes for Halloween if it makes you happy – just don't be going around trying to freak people out with your terrorist clothing.'

US military introduce Childbomber McChildbombface

An online poll conducted by the US Air Force to name its newest MQ-1 Predator drone has resulted in the $4m aircraft being christened *Childbomber McChildbombface*, it has emerged.

The comical monicker was chosen ahead of the preferred names, *Freedom Machine* and *Liberty Fire*, and moves made by the US Air Force to block the use of *Childbomber McChildbombface* were thwarted by a vicious online backlash.

The *Childbomber McChildbombface* fiasco mirrors the naming of the newest Royal Research Ship, which was saddled with *Boaty McBoatface* by hilarious people online.

'If they're going to deploy this weapon overseas despite widespread criticism of the drone programme, then at least we should get to name it,' said one member of the *Childbomber McChildbombface* campaign.

'We wish we could have named it *Nocollateralhumandamage McNocollateralhumandamageface*, but like the drones themselves, that's just not accurate.'

Childbomber McChildbombface is already operational in the Middle East, and so far has lived up to its name and then some.

US kills 26 civilians, successfully saving them from ISIS

The US government has proclaimed a historic victory in the fight against ISIS – a recent airstrike in Syria killed twenty-six innocent civilians, sparing them the fate of being killed by ISIS.

Forced into acknowledging their huge victory by on-the-ground monitoring agencies, who revealed that the twenty-six civilians were the sole casualties of a strategic strike against ISIS in the town of Al-Khan in Syria, the Obama administration stressed how fantastic a result the airstrike was.

At a White House press briefing a visibly agitated press secretary Josh Earnest chastised the US and international media for inferring that an airstrike that killed 26 innocent people could be viewed as a terrible tragedy that once again casts American foreign policy in a different, imperfect light.

'Jesus, how many times do I have to explain this to you guys? We killed them, yeah, but it means they weren't killed by ISIS, and that represents a huge victory in the war on terror,' Earnest explained to the assembled media while clutching his forehead in frustration.

Such utterances prompted further questions, much to the displeasure of the press secretary.

'Okay, dipshits. I'll say it again. These civilians were spared the horror of being killed by ISIS – you get that right? Or are you really, really stupid? We killed them, and the alternative to that was that they would be killed by ISIS, and I'm not hearing one of you saying "well done" or "good job".'

Muslim toddler arrested after crayon drawing sparks fears of giant woman attack

Homeland security officials in the United States today issued a yellow warning after a drawing by a Muslim child depicting some sort of monstrous over-sized woman was intercepted by elementary school teachers in Phoenix, Arizona.

Sa'id Ahmadi, 4, drew the picture during colouring hour and showed it to his teacher Annabel Harrison, who quickly became wary of what the chilling image might mean.

'It was a woman, but much larger than any other woman. Huge,

perhaps skyscraper-sized,' sobbed Harrison, a white woman.

'Given Sa'id's background, which I'm assuming is linked to the Middle East, I felt it necessary to raise the alarm. I kept Sa'id talking while a colleague called the FBI.'

The toddler from Phoenix, Arizona was detained for twenty-four hours as experts in terrorism grilled him to try to find out the meaning of the drawing.

'First off, stop calling him a toddler. That in there is a man,' said Special Agent Mike Long who headed up the investigation. 'That is a man who presented a clear danger to the security of those around him when he drew a picture depicting a woman with the ability to destroy us all. Where did he get the idea to draw that? Has he seen plans for this giant woman? Does she already exist? Is she about to be set loose in a major city? We need to know, now.'

Sa'id's family home has also been raided by Special Forces, and reports are coming in that they have found a fridge covered in similarly sinister images.

LEADER OF ISIS, ABU BAKR AL-BAGHDADI

AGE: 44

JOB: bad guy

KNOWN FOR: being the leader of terrorist group ISIS.

WHY IS HE IN THE NEWS: he's not really, actually. People are still talking about Kate Middleton's new haircut though.

DOES HE HAVE A HOOK FOR A HAND: sadly, no.

CHARACTERISTICS: indecisiveness: still hasn't settled on a name for ISIS, IS, Islamic State of Iraq and the Levant, Daesh.

DREAMS: Turning the world into a hellish extremist paradise. Landing the role of the next Bond villain.

SALARY: $100,000 plus expenses, and a pending virgins-in-heaven bonus.

HOBBIES: raping women, killing women, empowering disenfranchised and marginalised men so they too can rape and murder women. Also murders children and men. In case you're not picking up what we're putting down – he's an awful dose altogether.

TRUMP SPECIAL

Isis agrees to leave destruction of Western civilisation to Trump

A spokesperson for the Islamic State terrorist organisation has issued a statement saying that the group will call off their jihad against the West until after the US presidential election, to see if Donald Trump can save them a few quid on bullets and explosives.

Despite the lack of recent media coverage due to the Middle East being 'very meh' these days, ISIS – aka ISIL, aka the Bad Ones – are still very much active in several war-torn areas across the region.

Although their original plan was to draw their Western enemies into a 'final holy war', ISIS now believes the best way to destroy the West is to just sit back and hope Donald Trump, the Republican nomination, wins the US presidential election.

In the statement released today, ISIS puts its full support behind Trump, and has urges the American public to 'do the right thing for ISIS' when the time comes.

'Trump Akbar,' yelled a senior spokesperson for ISIS. 'There's no sense in us trying to take over the whole Middle East. There are only thirty thousand of us. Let Trump become president, leave him to his own devices, and he'll kick off a war with every Muslim in the world. He'll do all the radicalising for us, on his dollar.

Trump cancels Irish trip amid fears he might be related to some lad from Offaly

Presidential candidate Donald Trump has pulled out of a planned trip to Ireland this month after his security team revealed that some lad from Offaly is claiming he is a long-lost relative of the 70-year-old business tycoon.

Trump was scheduled to visit his County Clare hotel and country club next week, but has cancelled the trip in a bid to avoid being forced into a handshake and a hug with Niall Keenan, a 37-year-old from Harrismor, Offaly.

Keenan, with nothing better to do, traced Trump's family tree back almost six hundred years, and claims that the O'Trumps (as they were then known) and the Keenans share a bond through marriage.

Eager to avoid having to face the horrific experience that Barack Obama endured during his first term in office, Trump cancelled the trip in favour of going to a Klan rally in Arkansas.

'Mr Trump knows he's only one trip away from having a service station outside Tullamore named after him,' said one Republican advisor, 'so, he's making every effort to avoid contact with anyone claiming to be a relative,' He added, 'We've had Mr Keenan on a watch-list for some time now, and we'll be doing our best to keep him in Offaly, where he belongs.'

Robot from the future apprehended after trying to kill Donald Trump

The race for the Oval Office took an unexpected twist yesterday, when police apprehended a cyborg claiming to have been sent from the year 2045 on a mission to kill Republican nominee Donald Trump.

Appearing in the form of a well-built Caucasian male, the unit was spotted acting suspiciously outside the venue in New Hampshire, the state in which Mr Trump comfortably won the Republican vote earlier this year.

It took fourteen police officers to sedate and arrest what was believed to be an ordinary man, before the cyborg revealed itself to be an infiltration unit sent from the future on a desperate mission to save humanity from itself.

'We get like eight or nine of these things every year,' said Sgt Mike Kozlowski, speaking to the assembled press.

'People in the future keep sending robots back for one reason or another. This one kept screaming at us that we had to let him go, so that he could kill Donald Trump. Then he ranted about the future and some war with Mexico, billions dead, blah, blah, blah – the usual stuff.'

'These robots from the future are always going on about this apocalypse or that holocaust, and they always need to kill just one guy to prevent it. So we just follow standard procedure when we catch them; we throw them in the trash compactor out the back and carry on as normal.'

Donald Trump was unavailable for comment because he was busy thinking up more inflammatory things to say about minorities.

Iraqi army invades America to liberate its people from Donald Trump

They advanced under the cover of darkness, but make no mistake, the armed forces of the Republic of Iraq intended to bring light to the desperate people of America in their time of need, WWN reports from the frontline of the emerging conflict.

As emboldened tyrant Donald Trump further strengthened his position of power in America after securing more Republican primary victories, America's dire state of affairs led to one country intervening on behalf of the innocent citizens of the downtrodden Western nation.

'We know what is it like, and we were saved from it all in 2003. We can see the parallels and felt we must act,' explained General of the Iraqi Army Ali Kameni. 'Plus, once we heard Trump praise Saddam Hussein, we knew we had to act fast to save the people of America.'

Iraqi forces advanced on several key strategic locations across America early this morning, securing Trump Tower in New York as well as the Trump International Hotel in Las Vegas.

Kameni admitted he was overwhelmed by the emotional welcome they received from the oppressed people of America.

'Children in the streets openly weeping and hugging us; mothers giving us flowers – the people were so appreciative of the new found freedom we had bestowed upon them. I will never forget this moment,' Kameni told WWN, fighting back the tears.

While the liberation of the American people by the Iraqi Army is not yet complete, the most moving and perhaps enduring image so far is that of ordinary New Yorkers coming together to tear down a statue of Trump outside his Trump Tower building.

Joyous, tearful chants of 'down with Trump' were heard on the streets for hours afterwards.

TRUMP SPECIAL

Trump praised after opening fire on mosque with semi-automatic rifle

Republican presidential candidate Donald Trump received a huge surge in support today after an incident which saw him open fire on a mosque in Louisville, Kentucky, with a semi-automatic rifle earlier today.

Trump won widespread support and the Republican nomination on the basis of his promise to 'make America great again'.

Shortly after finishing a speech at a well-attended rally, Trump produced several guns from beneath the speaker's podium, including a semi-automatic rifle, to loud cheers and urged the crowd to follow him.

'This is going to be the best mass shooting of all time, believe you me. I'm going to do it,' Trump said to the large crowd that swelled behind him as he made his way to a nearby mosque.

Sustained bursts of fire from Trump's rifle shattered the window panels of the Golden Leaf Mosque on the outskirts of Louisville and a large number of casualties were reported by local news outlets.

Once the last of those attending afternoon prayers was killed Trump reloaded his rifle and with a spate of gunfire emblazoned his name on one of the outside walls of the mosque.

Despite the loss of life – estimates put the number of dead at forty-three – keen observers of the US presidential race have confirmed this mass shooting of American Muslims could well win Trump the upcoming election.

'He's hit upon all the vital conversation points for a lot of voters. He used a gun to kill some Muslims, and a cursory glance at the bodies and initial reports tells me some of the victims had the letters 'IS' in their names. In addition, some were possibly black, gay and also Syrian,' explained political commentator Ralph Feeder.

'It's a stroke of political genius, no doubt, and this is reflected in the 40 per cent boost in his popularity, and there's even talk of the Clinton campaign considering doing something similar just to stay within touching distance of Trump,' added columnist Stephen Beauchamps.

Hardline Republican supporters did, however, criticise the lack of Mexicans among the dead.

Trump is not expected to face criminal charges as all local police-force members were in attendance at the rally and came to the businessman's aid when his rifle jammed momentarily.

Donald Trump admits there are a lot of great ideas in *Mein Kampf*

American presidential candidate Donald Trump has admitted to drawing on the measured and reasoned writings of Adolf Hitler's manifesto *Mein Kampf* in an effort to find a solution to the 'Muslim problem'.

Speaking at a Republican rally, Trump endorsed proposals such as collating a database on US citizens who happen to be Muslim, and perhaps issuing them with a unique ID, much to the disgust of many American citizens.

'I'm going to come up with the best way of discriminating against a large group of people, believe you me. This guy Hitler, he had some good ideas, but he didn't go far enough. Let's make America great again,' Trump said to a surprisingly loud round of applause from the crowd.

Citing the threat posed by Syrian refugees and using made-up facts for the purposes of inciting hate and fear, Trump said he had leafed through his old first edition copy of *Mein Kampf* and admitted it was a great read, with a wealth of information and arguments.

'I mean, the guy was a socialist, let's not forget that, but he had one, maybe two, good ideas. Hitler tattooed large groups of troublesome people and rounded them up into prisons and camps – this is what we have to do,' Trump added.

Trump admitted, however, that he had a problem with the idea of applying a star to the clothes of Muslims living in America.

'I'd be happy to replace it with a Trump logo, that's a great branding opportunity, and maybe some giant 'X' or something through the word 'Muslim' – believe you me, this would solve everything,' Trump concluded.

TRUMP SPECIAL

America fucked

America has been branded 'completely fucked' today after news that Hillary Clinton has effectively clinched the Democratic nomination for US president.

Stuck between a rock and a hard place, American citizens are now being asked to vote for one of two incredibly wealthy people, both of whom have vested interests in a number of questionable corporations, questionable morals and possibly a series of undisclosed tax affairs too complex and expensive to investigate.

'I suppose I'll vote for whichever one appears to be the least corrupt after the campaign,' said one New Yorker today, who admitted he couldn't care less. 'Trump is bat-shit crazy, but Hillary is the spawn of Satan and cannot be trusted. You might as well be choosing between Saddam Hussein and Gaddafi.'

'There's 320 million people in this country, and this is the best we can do? We are truly fucked,' conceded another prospective voter.

Following the news of Clinton's nomination, hundreds of thousands of American citizens have begun applying for visas in the hope of emigrating from the North American country.

'I'm applying for a Russian visa,' said one man we met. 'Putin seems pretty grounded in comparison to these two megalomaniacs. Plus, Russia is way bigger than America too, and the people aren't so unhealthy. America was great while it lasted.'

The 2016 United States presidential election is the 58th quadrennial US presidential election, and probably the last.

AMERICAN NEWS

Obama officially done with America's bullshit

In a stirring address to the American people, a shattered-looking US President Barack Obama admitted his patience with Americans had been exhausted and confirmed he was 'done with their bullshit'.

'I tried, I really did, but you guys don't make it easy,' Obama said as he confirmed he was just going to lock himself away in the Oval Office until his presidential term was up in January.

In recent weeks, America has been affected by a number of high-profile tragedies involving firearms and the loss of life, which is something the president would have been able to deal with only for yet more bullshit to come along, causing him further distress.

'I had to endorse someone for president the other day who, if she wasn't who she is, would be in jail, and I had to do that because there's a nut-job in a toupee

trying to get hold of the nuclear codes,' said Obama passionately and rather sternly, his voice rising in anger.

'And a lot of you guys are voting for that wacko. I'm done, I'm frankly done with all your bullshit, America,' Obama added, now shouting.

Obama, a shadow of the figure who took office eight years ago, may have had the news of whistleblower Chelsea Manning's suicide attempt on his conscience too, or may have been feeling frustrated at Republicans' desire to restrict women's access to abortions and basic healthcare and their reluctance to update gun restrictions.

'This is officially someone else's mess to clean the fuck up,' Obama concluded, speaking of the greatest nation on earth.

WNN PROFILES

HILLARY CLINTON

AGE: 69

OCCUPATION: looking like your aunt who, try as she might, does an astonishingly poor job of being 'down with the kids'.

KNOWN FOR: being a former First Lady, standing by her man in such a way that completely convinced everyone she and her husband were deeply, totally in love and not just providing the creator of the Netflix show *House of Cards* with the basis for a show. Loving money and power.

LOVES: pretending she didn't consistently oppose gay rights and gay marriage until the point when she realised it would be advantageous for her to do a U-turn and suddenly support it. Money. She's not picky, she'll take it from anyone.

MOST LIKELY TO SAY: I agree – of course, I only agree if it gets me your vote.

LEAST LIKELY TO SAY: let's cut the shit, give me all the money and power you have.

DESIRES: to be president, not because she will make a great and distinguished leader but because no one should be president except for Hillary Clinton.

DONALD TRUMP

AGE: 70

HOBBIES: casual racism, telling more elaborate lies than a two-year-old caught overdosing on his secret supply of chocolate. Also, being sexually attracted to his daughter.

KNOWN FOR: having a rare inverted penis that causes him to lash out a lot. Wearing one of his ex-wives on his head as a toupee.

PERSONAL WEALTH: Donald Trump has the best personal wealth, believe you me. Let me tell you, he has all the big money.

MOST LIKELY TO: bring about a nuclear apocalypse.

LEAST LIKELY TO: use his two brain cells to make a statement that is devoid of monstrous stupidity.

CONTROVERSIES: numbering close to a million separate incidents at this point.

EXCLUSIVE

'Which one of you fucks do I need to promote?' – Clinton asks FBI interrogators

US presidential nominee Hillary Clinton breathed a sigh of relief this week after FBI Director James Comey confirmed he could not charge Clinton for using private email servers on which she transferred top-secret information while she was secretary of state, despite similar incidents garnering sanctions and criminal investigations.

Following a four-hour interrogation of the 69-year-old, Mr Comey was happy that the possible future president of the United States was just 'extremely careless', and should not face any federal charges.

During the FBI interview, Mrs Clinton, whose pockets were visibly bulging with money, asked interviewers what she had to do to dig herself out of the situation.

'So, which one of you fucks do I need to promote?' her transcript read. 'I've got some investors flying into Haiti in the morning so let's make this quick, yeah?'

Clinton went on to compliment her interrogators on a game well played, stating that their decision not to pursue criminal charges would see them rewarded in the event of Clinton becoming president later this year.

'This ain't your first rodeo, boys, is it? Smart move, I'll give you that,' Clinton remarked, fully aware that there was ample evidence contradicting her own accounts of her use of private email servers which could lead many to assert that Clinton had lied a nauseating number of times.

In response, one FBI interrogator stated the agency is 'caught between a rock and a hard place', pointing out previous instances in which American citizens were either exiled or prosecuted for breaches of security.

'Considering we've locked Chelsea Manning away for thirty-five years for leaking classified files, we could be in for some backlash here, Hillary,' said the interrogator. 'And I'm sure Snowdon will have a field day with this, but yeah, I could do with a pay bump, now that you mention it.'

Tense stand-off ends as Oregon militia return home to fuck their sisters

Just a few short days after seizing a federal building in Oregon, USA, an armed militia has stood down after realising that its members would be unable to have sex with their relations while the siege continued.

The group had been occupying part of the Malheur National Wildlife Refuge after exploiting a loophole in the American justice system which states that law enforcement officers are not allowed to use force against people clad in body armour carrying machine guns who storm a federal building in the event of those people being white.

Claiming to be protesting against the sentencing of a pair of ranchers convicted of poaching and arson, the group has been represented in interviews by well-known anti-government activist Ammon Bundy, who cannot be called a terrorist for reasons that are currently unclear.

Although the group claimed to be willing to stay entrenched for as long as was needed to have their demands met, many of the 150-strong militia began to file out of the government building after an agonising two days of not banging their sisters.

'It is our constitutional right as white Americans to walk around carrying automatic weapons and to seize buildings in an attempt to force our ideology on others,' said one protester, possibly called Chuck.

'With that being said, I haven't had me a piece of my sister in almost two days, so I'm off home. Take care, God bless America, and watch out for them Muslim bastards while you're at it.'

It is believed that the last of the holdouts will have cleared out by nightfall and will be enjoying some well-earned sister sex as soon as they've had a nice hot squirrel dinner.

Obama's new gun laws to limit gun owners to one murder per year

Representatives of America's right-wing Republican movement have reacted angrily to the news emerging from the White House that gun-carrying citizens will be limited to committing just one unlawful murder per year.

The news comes as President Barack Obama used executive powers to tighten up background checks and introduced several changes to gun laws in an effort to reduce the number of gun deaths across the United States.

While many Republicans and members of the vastly influential National Rifle Association in America have asserted their right to carry arms, Obama is set to limit the murder count, angering many.

'Seriously, just one? Across 365 days? What are our people going to shoot at for the rest of the year?' executive vice-president of the NRA, Wayne LaPierre, told the media in response to the news, while simultaneously firing his gun in the air.

'Just last month an innocent gun was shot by another gun, damaging it beyond repair. I've not heard one mention of that gun by the president, but sure, a few hundred people die and he won't shut up about it,' LaPierre added, bringing himself to tears as he recalled a Smith & Wesson 41 no longer with us.

Some individuals are even threatening use of lethal force to ensure their Second Amendment rights are secured and the news of a limit in the number of murders they can carry out could be the final straw.

'Too many know the tragedy of losing a loved one to gun violence and so I must reduce the number of murders each gun owner can carry out to just one per year,' President Obama said in his address to the American people. He then paused for a moment to squeeze one of his testicles as hard as he could in an effort to bring on some tears, which are so highly valued by the public and media alike.

Currently, there are next to no limits on the number of people gun owners can kill per year, and this sort of nanny state move by the White House may further heighten tensions between the authorities and those who plan on shooting someone.

Latest system update gives Clinton three more human expressions

The latest system update for synthetic humanoid robot The Clinton 2016 has been well received in tech circles with much of the praise focussed on the addition of three lifelike, almost human expressions.

The Clinton 2016, fondly referred to by its operators as Hillary Clinton, can now address humans and react to words, pictures and sounds with almost double the number of expressions available to the previous model.

'Oh, we're delighted. The Hillbot can now express mild appreciation, stern joy and effortless awkwardness,' its chief operator Robby Mook explained.

'While humanoid robots are a relatively new technology, we firmly believe that if someone with particularly poor eyesight saw this model they'd almost believe it was human.'

The robot, designed in America and assembled in a Chinese kindergarten, previously had a software patch fitted which allowed it to respond to questions quickly and to sycophantically agree with whatever opinion was expressed in order to become well liked by a human.

Not everyone is impressed with the latest update, however, and many people report feeling ill at ease and even nauseous at seeing a robot with human characteristics.

'I just don't trust it, it's a bit uncanny valley for me. And worst of all, you get the weird feeling it doesn't even know it's a robot,' shared tech sceptic and Florida native Will Orphen.

Rescue mission launched as thousands stranded on higher moral ground

A worldwide rescue mission has been launched today after thousands of internet commentators were left stranded on higher moral ground in dangerously ignorant conditions, following an incident in Cincinnati Zoo in which a gorilla was shot in a bid to protect a young boy.

Internet rescue service personnel have been inundated with emergency calls from people trapped in comment sections, many of them incredibly passionate about stories that they can jump to conclusions about without reading the facts.

'It's very hard to gain access to the higher moral ground. It's tough for rescuers to get past the raging statements made without even a cursory look at the information, and conditions overhead aren't great as we've to weather a torrent of mindless abuse,' explained lead rescuer Don Franklin.

In fact, several panicked victims resorted to lambasting the parents of the child in question in a bid to survive the gushing stream of opinions engulfing social media.

'Could I wait until the information is gathered before forming an opinion? Of course, but where's the fun in that, plus they're African American and the father also has a criminal record: I read it in the *Mail Online*,' said one man who has been trapped on the moral high ground since Saturday. 'What kind of neglectful parent brings their kids to the zoo like that anyway? Surely there's a law preventing people who have spent time in cages from visiting animals in cages?'

Many experts in the field of ape psychology have since come forward to point out that it would obviously have been safer to have allowed the child to be dragged underwater by an eight-hundred pound gorilla that has spent most of its incarcerated life in cramped conditions while being stared at by noisy humans with flashing camera phones.

'Split-second decisions made in high-pressure situations to protect children are my bread and butter, so trust me when I say I know exactly what they should have done in that moment. I'm livid the zoo didn't contact me,' shared Alan Boland from Waterford, a father of none and avid nature programme fan.

'That poor animal should have been talked down using bananas and sign language. All gorillas know sign language and they should have coaxed him away from the child with bananas. Simple,' he concluded.

If you have been affected by a gorilla tragedy, please leave your comment below. If you have not been affected by a gorilla tragedy, do not let that stop you.

HARAMBE

AGE: 17

KNOWN FOR: proving humans have infinitely more interest in the plight of one gorilla than in other pressing issues, such as the 65 million refugees displaced across the globe.

THANKFUL FOR: the fact his death was not in vain as he would be happy to learn he became the centre of a thousand viral stories for a few days.

MOST HUMAN QUALITY: was going to kill a child for misbehaving.

LEAST HUMAN QUALITY: didn't have an opinion which took the form of a lengthy rant on his Facebook account about how bad and irresponsible parents at the zoo can be.

LASTING LEGACY: made people forget about Cecil the lion. Will be played by Benedict Cumberbatch in a movie about his life.

BREXIT SPECIAL

Fuckin' gobshites

Britain is making headlines around the world today after more than seventeen million gobshites did something rather stupid.

YouGov, a market research company which specialises in exit polls, confirmed that the biggest winners of the referendum, which saw Britain vote to leave the EU, turned out to be ignorance, casual racism and Nigel Farage's erection.

Many voters were swayed by the fact that a Leave vote would supposedly bring day-to-day decision-making powers back into the hands of elected members of the British Parliament, and away from the unelected bureaucrats in the EU.

However, thanks to a successful Leave campaign, an unelected replacement for David Cameron will first have to be chosen and then verified by the unelected queen before Britain gets to the business of regaining the £150 billion wiped off their economy since trading opened this morning.

Leave campaigner and utter bastard Nigel Farage confirmed that any financial hardship people could face in the years to come will be mitigated by the fact that dirty foreigners won't be flooding into Britain and contributing positively to society and the economy.

On the recommendation of Donald Trump, among others, 52 per cent of those who turned out ignored an overwhelming number of experts to exercise their right to vote in a fit of misguided jingoistic silliness. While many people had legitimate concerns about Britain's place within the EU and the overall benefit of remaining a member, the vast majority of those voting had a deep-seated desire to just see how 'fucked up things could get'.

'Fuckin' gobshites,' the majority of Europe confirmed upon waking up to the news that Britain had voted to exit the EU.

In his resignation speech a surprised David Cameron confirmed, 'I will resign, but if I'm being honest, I thought if anything was going to bring me down it was going to be that whole fucking dead pig thing.'

BREAKING NEWS

Thousands of British refugees make dangerous journey across the Irish Sea

The Irish coastguard has today issued a nationwide warning for the east coast as hundreds of thousands of British refugees risk their lives to cross the Irish sea in an attempt to flee the impoverished and unstable nation.

Dinghies overflowing with desperate migrants are so far halfway through their journey, many with women and children aboard, all wishing to make a new start on the Emerald Isle.

'We have rescued hundreds of people from crafts due to overcrowding,' winchman Derek Ryan of Rescue 117 told WWN today. 'It's a terrible situation as many of these people are only hoping for a better quality of life in the EU.'

Taoiseach Enda Kenny has called an emergency meeting in the Dáil this afternoon to help find a solution to the influx of British refugees. It is expected many of those landing on the Irish coast will have to be quarantined, as they are not a part of the European Union.

'Emergency prefabs will be erected to help house these poor unfortunate people,' Mr Kenny stated. 'I urge everyone to do what they can to help support the migrants in any way, whether that be waiting with hot cups of tea on the shoreline, or giving them fresh clothes to wear.'

An estimated 450,000 people have already fled the UK mainland to neighbouring EU countries.

Financial pearls of wisdom from Economics Correspondent Freddy Nobbs

When asking your boss for a pay rise, it always helps to be holding a weapon of some sort. I'd pick a hammer myself.

'We'll Take Scotland Too. But Not Wales. Fuck Wales' – Taoiseach Enda Kenny

Taoiseach Enda Kenny has for the first time opened the door to a future referendum on Irish unity with Northern Ireland and mentioned the possibility of taking on Scotland too, but not Wales, WWN can reveal.

Speaking with his mouth, Kenny drew comparisons with the situation in Germany after the fall of the Berlin Wall in 1990.

'This is exactly like that time,' he said. 'We'll be like the Germans in a few years – financing a string of countries we don't really care for while imposing our own ideals and financial structures on them to suit ourselves. Northern Ireland is ours for the taking. Scotland too. But not Wales. Fuck Wales. Those lads are muck savages.'

In a significant move, Mr Kenny warned the European Union to prepare for the prospect of Northern Ireland and Scotland seeking to join the Republic, and said that he proposes to call the new grouping the Irish Union.

'We're open to talks with the Isle Of Man, Isle of Wight, the Falklands, Rory McIlroy – basically we'll adopt whoever wants us,' added the Taoiseach. 'I just want to emphasise again that Wales is not wanted in the Irish Union. Besides, there's not enough room for two ridiculous languages.'

Brexit: How it will affect your upcoming abortion

Frightened young women all across Ireland woke up today with yet another thing to worry about – how Britain's decision to leave the European Union will impact on their upcoming abortion.

'I'm scheduled to head over to Liverpool next Friday ... is my passport still okay?' asked Silé O'Hanlin, a 17-year-old girl who fell pregnant after a rape at a house party. 'I've already spent the last three weeks crying, and I could only afford the trip by dropping out of school and getting a job in the local newsagents ... I read online that the pound is in trouble ... does that mean the price of the procedure is going to go up?'

Sentiments such as these were echoed among the estimated three hundred women who were making the trip to England this month to avail of services that are unavailable in Ireland.

Women carrying babies with fatal foetal abnormalities, or going through unplanned or unwanted pregnancies were forced to shoulder extra stress as the ramifications of Brexit played out before their eyes. However, in a statement from the HSE, women were reassured that although Britain had opted to pull the trigger of a shotgun aimed at its own head, it hadn't lost the plot to the degree that it was denying women autonomy over their own bodies.

'Abortion services are still available in Britain,' said an HSE spokesperson.

'You don't have to worry that the country has devolved into some sort of backwards-thinking hellhole that treats women like second-class citizens. If you can get yourself over to England, they'll still sort you out.'

Meanwhile the Irish government is praying that the current abortion laws in Britain remain unchanged, otherwise they may have to finally stop ignoring calls to repeal the 8th Amendment.

BREXIT SPECIAL

Queen officially hands Northern Ireland back to Ireland in emotional ceremony

Britain's Queen Elizabeth II has today officially handed the deeds to Northern Ireland back to the Republic of Ireland, in one of the most memorable and emotional ceremonies of the past one hundred years.

Flanked by party leaders from both sides of the border, the 90-year-old monarch thanked the people of Northern Ireland for remaining under British rule for so long, and apologised to their Republic counterparts for all the atrocities over the past seventy years.

'Our proud nations have been through thick and thin together,' the teary-eyed queen began as, in the background, a montage of black-and-white pictures depicted Northern Ireland's civil rights struggle and violent past. 'So forgive me if I appear a little emotional – it has been a long road for everyone here. It is my honour to hand over the six counties of Antrim, Armagh, Down, Fermanagh, Londonderry, Tyrone and all their financial woes to the Republic of Ireland.'

Receiving the deeds to the now former part of the United Kingdom, Taoiseach Enda Kenny echoed Queen Elizabeth's words, before thanking her for finally releasing Northern Ireland back to Ireland.

'Eh, now hang on a second there, Liz,' a panicked-looking Fine Gael leader said as the queen exited the ceremonial stage and hopped into a waiting car, moving quicker than expected for a 90-year-old. 'I was told I was just being invited up for tea and biscuits. What if we don't want it back?" Kenny continued, now dripping with a mixture of tears and sweat.

'We've been tricked. I fucking told you this would happen,' Kenny whispered to an aide as Gerry Adams rushed the stage in a failed attempt to prise the deeds from the Taoiseach's hands.

Moments before, Prince Phillip had been seen comforting the emotional queen while attempting to ease the transfer of ownership by commenting on a foreign-looking man in the audience, and calling Enda Kenny an 'empty-headed, bog-dwelling neanderthal'.

EU asks Britain if it's fucking going or not

'You know how you'll be at a house party and someone will say they're leaving, and then a half-hour later you see them still chatting away to people while drinking all the cans? It's like that,' said Angela Merkel today, speaking about Britain's refusal to take forward the Brexit promised in June.

Markets and political institutions were rocked by Great Britain's decision to leave the EU, which resulted in a number of politicians stepping down, including Prime Minister David Cameron.

However, more than three months later, Britain has yet to shut down its borders or cut itself free from daily EU dealings, prompting higher-ups in the European Union to ask if the British are really leaving and, if so, when.

'Get out or come in, just don't stand there with the door open, letting the fucking heat out,' said Merkel, who has appointed herself 'Mrs Europe' for the time being.

'This thing of saying you're off, but lingering for months is just annoying. I used to go out with someone like that – oh, I have to go, I have work tomorrow blah blah blah – and then they'd still be there two hours later just talking shite. Go. Leave. Adios. Buh-bye.'

Meanwhile, Michael Gove, Boris Johnson and Nigel Farage have all agreed never to speak of the Leave campaign again, in the hopes that people forget all about it.

BREXIT SPECIAL

5 Reasons why Jeremy Corbyn is the antichrist

UK Labour leader Jeremy Corbyn has been causing a stir in Britain by expressing controversial views that have not been pre-approved by the ruling Conservative government, rich people or even Tony Blair.

Here at WWN, with the help of the *Daily Mail*, we have compiled five of the most devastating stances which prove Corbyn is the antichrist:

1. 'I want to murder the Queen and make Gerry Adams the prime minister'

(Jeremy Corbyn, 23 March, 1933) There it is, in the man's own words. We don't feel there is much to add other than to point out that the devil should present himself to the nearest police station immediately.

2. He is against war.
Corbyn's disgusting anti-war stance would prove devastating to the economy, costing British weapons manufacturers billions of pounds in profits. If Corbyn was to assume power in Britain, his pre-apocalyptic tyrannical rule would see the end of arms dealers selling weapons in nineteen countries known to use child soldiers or target children according to the UN. Disgusting.

3. Corbyn is pro anti-.
The grey-haired bastard is literally for being against a lot of things: Trident, social inequality, poverty, working 24/7. You name it, Jezzer opposes it. Britain would be wise to shift its focus away from a badger cull to a Corbyn cull if it doesn't want its grandchildren speaking Muslim.

4. He once held up people on the Tube to offer his seat to a pregnant lady.
People. Heading to work. Had to wait twelve agonising seconds as Mr Shit himself stood in their way in order to vacate his seat and give it to a heavily pregnant woman. While eyewitnesses were thin on the ground, speculation suggests she was a foreigner.

5. Has never seen Downton Abbey.
Not once. Not fucking once has he watched the beloved ITV drama. Corbyn has no idea what Anna and Mr Bates have been through. What a bastard.

Prince George orders execution of classmates during first day at school

It was a busy day yesterday for Britain's Prince George as he began his first day at preschool, marked by a carefully choreographed photograph which made its way around the world.

His parents Prince William and Kate Middleton have said in the past that they hope to ensure their children have a normal upbringing, and interacting with other young members of the public was set to serve that purpose.

However, if media reports are to be believed, the future king grew immediately tired of his loyal toddler subjects as some had the audacity to answer questions posed by his teacher before he was able to even put his hand up.

'He's sort of used to being the centre of attention, and being told he'll rule over all these little shits one day, so I think he got quite cranky early on,' a Buckingham Palace insider explained to WWN.

'He started shouting, "I want to go home" but when a classmate said, "We don't go home until 2 p.m." he completely lost his shit, and ordered the execution of everyone in the room,' the insider added.

The execution of sixteen of George's fellow pupils has been described as 'regretful' by the royal family as William and Kate had struggled to find a decent pre-school in their locality and now none of his classmates are left alive.

The search for a new school begins again.

Tony Blair is an absolute cunt, finds Chilcot report

Shocking details emerging from the recently published Chilcot report into the war in Iraq have provoked an opinion never aired before regarding former British Prime Minister Tony Blair.

Weighing up all the information gathered during the course of his investigation, Sir John Chilcot found Blair to be 'an irredeemable and unremitting cunt of a man'.

'There can be no doubt, when leafing through the report, that the big takeaway from this is that Tony is really up there with the top cunts – I wouldn't hesitate in suggesting that he's a world-class cunt,' respected political commentator Francis Stoppard shared with WWN.

Tony Blair, the former Labour leader, was judged by the Chilcot report to have presented 'with a certainty that was not justified, to the British parliament and people, that Iraq had the capability of building and using weapons of mass destruction.'

The former PM also ignored warnings about the consequences of entering into a war with Iraq and even changed his rationale for invading Iraq after the fact, thus providing Chilcot with a solid basis for judging Blair to be a 'cunt of epic standing'.

'The c-word gets bandied about a lot when talking about world leaders who blindly enter into a war without much respect for things like assessments, facts, plans or human life, but no one can deny that Tony has really earned the title,' political commentator Stoppard added.

Blair was unavailable for comment, as it is believed he was busy being paid to help curry favour in the West for some heinous regime or dictator, in exchange for cash.

BRITISH NEWS

UKIP announce Faisal Umar Khan as new leader

UKIP has wasted no time in announcing a successor to outgoing leader Nigel Farage, with relative unknown Faisal Umar Khan being handed the task of continuing to help the party to grow amongst disenfranchised voters.

Khan, whose parents emigrated to the UK from Pakistan in 1964, was presented to the waiting press shortly after Farage's announcement that he would be stepping down.

'While Nigel achieved so much with UKIP, culminating in the successful Leave campaign, we do feel that now he's stepped aside, we need to take the party in a new, entirely different direction,' UKIP party chairman Steven Crowther shared with WWN.

'Our selection process for Nigel's successor has been second to

none, and in Faisal we have a qualified doctor, who went on to start several successful businesses while somehow finding the time to study for a Masters in politics. He's an impressive individual, the like of which you rarely see in England,' Crowther said, visibly excited by the 46-year-old Muslim's appointment.

Khan, an MP for Dudley, has edged out more prominent candidates for the leadership owing to his strong business ties to Pakistan and Middle Eastern countries, which will prove invaluable as Britain comes to terms with its future outside the EU.

'What attracted me to UKIP was their offer to allow me change their direction slightly, and I am only too happy to see they have agreed to my request of weekly

meetings in my local mosque and, starting next year, a number of my new colleagues have said they will partake in Ramadan as an act of solidarity,' Khan shared.

The businessman is also expected to aggressively pursue the fastest growing voting block in England, the British-Asian community.

'If we have cynically changed our policies to gain more votes from those communities, that is something we'll have to look into,' Khan said in one exchange, responding to a question on whether UKIP MPs should learn to speak Urdu, Arabic or even Romanian.

BREAKING NEWS

Human dies after being passed around under water by dolphins

There were terrifying and sad scenes on an Argentinian beach earlier today after members of the seemingly intelligent dolphin community claimed the life of one human.

Onlookers described how a young man in his twenties was happily swimming in shallow water when a dolphin dragged him further out to sea, keen to show off the exotic discovery to his dolphin friends.

'Dolphins are supposedly really smart, but they just kept passing him around underwater for about thirty minutes. Every dolphin in the sea wanted to get a look at him and hold him. He was dead after like five minutes – stupid fucking dolphins,' eyewitness Rodrigo Palacio explained to WWN.

What made the incident more tragic was that the victim, 27-year-old Carlos Bacara, was one of just seven billion remaining humans left on the planet. His death serves as yet another blow to the endangered human species.

Rumours are circulating that the dolphins had been curious to see what a human looks like after a recent incident saw a large group of vapid and vacuous humans drag a dolphin out of the sea in Argentina in order to pass it around for important selfie opportunities, ultimately leading to the completely avoidable death of the animal.

'The dolphins are actually more intelligent than we give them credit for,' explained the policeman charged with investigating the human death, Gabriel Banega. 'They uploaded several pictures of the victim to Instagram with the caption, "So this is what the dumbest fucking thing on the planet looks like".'

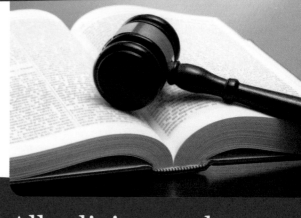

All religions to be banned under new common sense laws

A series of laws ratified by world leaders this week at a UN summit in New York has brought about an unprecedented change in the constitutions and laws that govern countries around the world.

In an effort to stem all current conflicts occurring across the world today, over 170 world leaders have signed up to an outright banning of all religions, citing 'common sense' as the main driving force behind the move.

'It's just common fucking sense, guys,' Russian premier Vladimir Putin told assembled media as he signed on the dotted line.

While the decision initially provoked an outcry from the citizenry of a number of nations, the benefit of such laws soon became obvious to them once the laws were administered.

'Ah, it's class, I'm getting on much better with the Prod next door, now that he's not a Prod, and I'm not a Catholic. Had him over for dinner last night and everything, and we had a great time. He has good taste in wine, too,' Belfast native Eoghan O'Connell revealed to WWN.

The laws are effective immediately and will be slowly phased in around the world, with all organised religions forced to dissolve and donate their income and assets to a common funding pool that will aid those in need.

Speaking after signing the historic unilateral agreements, US President Barack Obama cut a happy and relieved figure. 'This makes everyone's job a lot easier. We've scaled back on all foreign-led military operations now those Muslim lads – eh, I guess they're just "people" now? – those people lads no longer possess a divinely inspired hatred of us and vice versa.'

LIFESTYLE

'AND THEY SAY I DIDN'T HAVE A TALENT ... TRY BALANCING A CHAMPAGNE GLASS ON YOUR ASS. LOL.'

Fucking hero out running in the rain

Motorists sitting in traffic on the North Circular Road in Dublin this morning rolled down their windows and gave a slow clap to one 'goddamn hero' who was out running at 7.45 a.m. despite the fact that it was lashing rain.

'Oh, look at you, having your run without a care for the weather,' said one white van driver, giving the thumbs-up to the passing jogger.

Inspirational Quote of the Year

'You have to look through the rain to see the rainbow. Seriously, how much do you suck at life that seeing a rainbow is a really hard thing for you to do?'

'Aren't you just brilliant with your running, and in the rain too. You don't let things like rain get in the way of your fitness regime, do you? You don't make plans to get in shape for the New Year and then abandon those plans the first time you look out the window and see that it's a bit nippy out. You really are better than the rest of us. Keep it up.'

A social-media campaign was later launched to find the identity of the man, believed to be in his mid-twenties and described as being 'so, so, so healthy and fit'.

'Anyone know who the total legend was who was running this morning in the rain?' read the Facebook post on the newly created page entitled 'Look at this fucking hero'.

'Just would not stop running, even though his clothes and shoes and socks must have been soaking. Kept jogging in place while waiting on traffic lights too. Wow. Well done. No heart problems for him, eh?'

It remains to be seen whether or not the rock star will be out jogging in the rain tomorrow morning, but many are betting that he won't miss his daily opportunity to rub his fitness dedication levels in everyone's faces again.

WWN was granted exclusive access to a photoshoot earlier this week, in which a 4-year-old greyhound hit back at critics who claimed she was 'too skinny' on social media.

'I'm just naturally skinny,' said local greyhound, Skipper, as camera bulbs flashed all around her. 'I like to exercise, and some people just can't handle that.'

Greyhound defies 'skinny-shaming' critics in brave photoshoot

Skipper, who is a very good dog, was horrified to return from walkies in the park to find pictures of herself on Instagram and Twitter with captions claiming that she 'must have an eating disorder' and that she 'needed to go and get a good big bowl of Pedigree Chum for herself'.

'"Look at this skinny bitch" – that was the most common thing people were saying,' said Skipper, who worked hard to regain her figure after giving birth to a litter of fourteen. 'People can be as cruel when they're talking about slim dogs as they can when talking about overweight dogs. People see a pug waddling along and say, 'Oh, good for him, he's confident and curvy.' Then they look at me and say I'm disgusting because you can see my ribs.

'These photos will show that I'm perfectly comfortable with my body shape, and anyone that doesn't like it can sniff my last lamppost,' she concluded, before sprinting away.

Irish people asked to explain what they mean by 'sure you know yourself'

The time when an Irish person could simultaneously dodge a question and answer it may be coming to a close, as an international court ruling has demanded an explanation for the expression 'sure you know yourself'.

For decades, people from all across Ireland have skilfully steered conversations to their liking by simply responding to any question or query with the catch-all phrase.

'Sure you know yourself', originally coined by Michael Collins in 1921 when someone asked him how he got on in England, is both an answer to a question and a deflection: something no other phrase in the English language can lay claim to.

However, overuse of the phrase in recent times has led to a UN ruling that either the statement be explained in full, or struck from use altogether.

'No, we don't know ourselves,' said Mbutu Costello, chief spokesperson for the UN Nonsense Deactivation Committee. 'Please replace this statement with one that makes sense. You can't just keep using it in conversation while acting like it makes sense. We appreciate that it's easy to withhold information about yourself by dodging direct questions with a nonsensical phrase, but it's annoying and nobody likes it.'

The Irish government is to fight the ruling, stating that it is every Irish citizen's right to be able to tell people to mind their own fucking business without sounding rude.

Average teacher to receive 37 scented candles from students this year

Teachers across the country are bracing themselves for a flood of scented candles as school terms draw to a close and parents rush to make sure their child isn't the only kid who doesn't bring in a gift to school.

The giving of gifts to teachers can be traced to a Dublin school in the early 2000s, when one 8-year-old brought a box of Milk Tray into his Second Class teacher.

After every child in the classroom went home and told their parents, the same teacher received dozens of boxes of Milk Tray the following year, as parents feared that their child might not get as much education if they were the only one who didn't give the teacher anything at Christmas.

This trend soon spread to the whole school, and then to schools in the surrounding area before becoming a countrywide epidemic. Statistics show that parents are more likely to buy a scented candle for their kids' teacher, as it is a relatively universal gift that requires little or no actual thought.

'What was once a kind gesture is now a mandatory part of the education system,' said Hillary Martin, spokesperson for the Irish Teachers Association.

'All parents are duty-bound to give a gift valued at no less than €20 to their kids' teacher, regardless of how that teacher is performing in their job. Yankee Candles are the most common present, and teachers receive more of these than they could possibly burn in a year. They just pile up. On average, teachers have more candles in their house than the nearest cathedral.'

Meanwhile, experts in the art of cop-on have suggested that the phenomenon of giving gifts to teachers could be eradicated if parents would just agree that the whole thing was nonsense and that there's enough to be worried about at Christmas without fretting that your child is going to be singled out for the rest of the year if they don't buy their teacher a candle that smells like washing powder.

Bowl only fit for the bin after Weetabix left in it for ten minutes

A Carlow man has conceded that his favourite cereal bowl is now only fit for the bin after making the crucial error of not rinsing it immediately after eating his Weetabix this morning.

Kevin McCarroll, 27, left his bowl unattended for as little as ten minutes this morning after suffering from a sudden need that came out of nowhere to go have a bowel movement.

As the minutes passed, the remnants of Weetabix fused with the porcelain of McCarroll's *Breaking Bad* 'Los Pollos Hermanos' novelty cereal bowl, forming a bond that no amount of scalding water, Fairy Liquid or elbow grease could break.

The bowl, a gift to McCarroll from his girlfriend last Christmas, had to be put out of its misery after a half hour of frantic scrubbing failed to budge even the slightest bit of Weetabix.

'Let my tragedy be a warning to you all,' said a visibly moved McCarroll at a press conference later that day.

'You cannot leave a cereal bowl for even a minute without rinsing it out. Weetabix, porridge, cornflakes, it doesn't matter – the cereal will become welded to your favourite bowl in no time, and there's nothing you can do after that.'

Every year in Ireland thousands of bowls are thrown in the bin after their owners leave them unrinsed. To date, scientists have yet to find a stronger bonding material for smooth ceramics than dried-on Weetabix.

Boyfriend's excitement short-lived as girlfriend gets down on her knees, but proposes instead

A County Waterford man's dream was shattered this morning after long-time girlfriend Tracey Kent finally got down on her knees, but made a marriage proposal instead.

Tommy Bishop, 36, was left 'bewildered' by the request and said he had no other choice but to say yes as 'the guilt got the better of me'.

'I thought she was gonna give me something to smile about before going into work!' he recalled. 'All I got was this stupid ring and a promise. The lads are gonna slag the shite out of me now,' he added.

Mr Bishop has been going out with his girlfriend for six years and told WWN that he never wanted to get married to anyone because of financial concerns.

'Marriage is like betting someone half your shit that you'll stay with them forever,' he explained. 'I think it's time to open a sneaky bank account!'

Twenty-ninth February is traditionally said to be the only time a woman can propose to their man, an age-old tradition dating back to the ninth century.

Hotels and golf courses reported a vast increase in the number of

bookings on the day as thousands of men made arrangements for 'work-related day trips' to different parts of the country.

'We haven't seen this much business on a Wednesday in a long, long time,' said Mount Juliet Golf Course Manager David Keane. 'We've had a lot of members handing in their phones to reception and asking us to hold on to them until tomorrow.'

It is estimated over three hundred women make marriage proposals in Ireland on 29 February.

The Year in Stats

100% of friends who speak Irish to each other in public think they're fucking great.

Incredibly boring man doesn't need alcohol to have a good time

An incredibly boring Waterford man doesn't need alcohol to have a good time, it has been alleged.

Tommy Martin, a 29-year-old non-drinker, has been boring the pants off friends and family with the suggestion that he has a very enjoyable social life despite refraining from alcohol consumption.

'The dry shite has been going on about getting up before 1 p.m. on the weekends. I fall asleep mid-sentence listening to the cunt,' shared a friend of Tommy's, Alan Rattigan.

Despite claims of partaking in rock climbing, kayaking, running and enjoying something called a 'brunch' all before many of his friends wake up, Tommy has been able to provide little evidence that he is actually having anything normal, fun people call 'craic'.

'He's lost the run of himself. I don't like looking at a friend and saying, "You know what? I couldn't tell you the last time you yelled out SHOTS SHOTS SHOTS" in the middle of a pub. And this prick is trying to tell me he knows how to have fun?' professional banter merchant Cian Grogan explained to WWN.

'He's always cracking jokes on nights out, asking after my family and how things are going at work. It's like, stop trying to wreck the buzz and down a Jägerbomb already,' Cian confirmed.

Friends of Tommy's have also confirmed that if they get one more text from him 'looking to do something' before 5 p.m. on the weekends, they will snap.

Waterford mother acting like she's the one who got 600 points

A Waterford mother has made the fatal error of assuming that the 600 points received by her daughter in the Leaving Cert this year are transferable to her, WWN has learned.

Norah O'Farrelly, 56, an Ardmore native, has taken to carrying herself with the sort of satisfaction, pride and confidence normally reserved for 17- and 18- year-olds who have the world at their feet, after securing an impressive 600 points.

'Did you hear?' O'Farrelly said, standing beside the wall outside her house, where she had been patiently waiting for neighbours, or anyone, to walk by. 'We got 600 points.'

Careful to use the word 'we' when describing the success gained by her daughter Siofra through a process of hard work and more hard work, the mother's pride in her daughter's results was only eclipsed by the intoxicating feeling derived from acting as if she herself had got them.

'God, I couldn't do it all again, not if you paid me all the money in the world,' O'Farrelly remarked to friends in a Facebook status post, which read like the 56-year-old sat through exams in English, Maths, Irish, Biology, Economics, French and History.

'Finally getting a chance to let the hair down after all that stress and hard work #champagne,' confirmed O'Farrelly, who has no time to say 'well done' to her daughter as her own boasting commitments are set to keep her busy for the next few weeks.

HEALTH AND SCIENCE

Scientists confirm link between having a tiny penis and joining ISIS

Scientists have produced overwhelming proof that men joining terrorist group ISIS have comically small penises, WWN has learned.

'At first we thought it was just a coincidence, but we couldn't ignore how little there was of each and every member's member,' Professor Bryan J. Gilligunn shared with WWN.

While it is well known that ISIS had long since abandoned trying to recruit well-adjusted people who know how to read a book and not turn it into an excuse to murder, rape and pillage, this latest scientific research confirms ISIS have also limited their recruiting to lads with tiny lads.

'The members' cry of "Allahu Akbar" moments before carrying out an atrocity now actually seems more like a cry for help; a cry for help for their monumentally miniscule penises,' Professor Gilligunn shared with WWN.

Despite trying to remain professional at all times during their research, scientists broke down in tears of laughter as 99.5 per cent of all ISIS members exhibited tiny members.

'We had to spend a lot of money on more powerful microscopes as their genitals were barely visible to the naked eye,' Professor Gilligunn confirmed.

This research confirms the theory that people drawn to ISIS often have extreme views, psychotic tendencies, and a propensity to masturbate using tweezers.

Fitness Tips from Expert Fiachra Burley

Take steroids. Yes, your penis will shrivel up until it looks like a peanut in a sea of pubic hair, but just think of how ripped you'll look.

BREAKING NEWS

Mother not vaccinating child because she read something somewhere

A Waterford mother has confirmed her intention to leave her children unvaccinated against a series of infections and ailments thanks to the timely discovery of revelatory information she sort of remembers reading somewhere at some point in the last few weeks.

'There's all sorts of stuff in them vaccines, and they cripple a child on the spot,' explained mother-of-two Vicky Townsend to her GP, Dr Angela Cummings.

While the precise content of the Facebook post that whizzed by in her news feed is now only a hazy recollection of half-remembered things, Townsend isn't letting 'a single fucking vaccine' near her precious kids.

'All due respect to you being a doctor and all, but this post had loads of writing on it and a big 'X' sign through a vaccine, and then there was a sad-looking baby who was crying on it as well,' Townsend explained, detailing her tirelessly researched, peer-shared Facebook post.

Reminded that immunising her child against things like diphtheria, polio meningitis, septicaemia and pneumonia was a necessary and worthwhile thing to do, Townsend once again stressed how the evidence to the contrary was overwhelming.

'This other post had the word "mercury" in it – you get that, right? Like you know that's bad? Am I talking to a brick fucking wall here, doc, no disrespect like,' Townsend confirmed, safe in the knowledge that her children would not be brainwashed by mind-controlling autism bullets.

'Stop making tea wrong' people who add the milk first told

Scientists unable to explain continued shrinking of chocolate bars

Yet another annual Scientists For Chocolate Bar Shrinkage Research (SFCBSR) Conference has yielded no fresh insight into the mysterious shrinking of chocolate bars here in Ireland and abroad, WWN has learned.

A packed 3Arena played host to a range of the world's most prominent scientists who share a passion for chocolate bars as well as a mutual disgust at their inexplicable shrinking, which has increased tenfold in recent years.

'I have deferred all my clinical trials and research relating to a cure for serious cancers in a bid to solve this distressing phenomenon,' keynote speaker at this year's SFCBSR conference Dr Helena Gunctfeld explained to WWN.

Confusion was first expressed by Irish scientist and chocolate-eater Noel Brogan, who noticed that between 1999 and 2015 the average chocolate bar shrunk in size by forty-three inches.

'We must, first off, commend chocolatiers who are at just as much of a loss as ourselves to explain why the bars have got smaller. They really want to solve this too. But, despite the cooperation we're no closer to finding out why Dairy Milk, Mars Bars and Toffee Crisps have all shrunk so rapidly in recent years,' Dr Gunctfeld added.

Tests carried out on 14,000 varieties of cocoa bean reveal that the beans have seen no change recently.

'Oh God, eh, yeah, so very frustrating,' explained chief chocolate-bar designer at Cadbury, Matthew Gerrard. 'It's like "ah, if only we could get to the bottom of this". We're just as mad as our customers are, honestly,' Gerrard added, raising his fist in mock anger.

'We just measured our tins of Roses this year and they've got smaller again. Naturally, we're devastated, but nothing has changed on the production line. Honest!' Gerrard concluded.

A strict set of regulations has been issued to a dissident group of tea makers in Ireland, who have flouted the well-established rules on the method for making the hot beverage.

A nationwide education drive, funded by the Department of Education, has been rolled out today in an effort to bring an end to the anarchy visited upon kitchens and kettles across the country by a small but growing number of tea-illiterate citizens.

'The Milk First Movement is only a fraction below ISIS and the IRA in our list of threats to Ireland,' admitted a high-ranking source in the Irish army. 'Some people want to continue to make Ireland great, and you can't do that without making a proper cup of tea, but the MFM are sadistic bastards and they don't seem to even care they're doing it wrong.'

The MFM group, which has a loose assembly of members, is dedicated to putting milk in a cup of tea before a tea bag or hot water is even in there. This method has been known to cause great upset to normal people when they catch sight of the bizarre and irresponsible practice.

'We must end this, and the only way to do that is through education,' explained head of the Put The Milk In Last Campaign, President of Ireland, Michael D. Higgins.

The President, along with other famous faces, will carry out nationwide demonstrations in schools and public spaces in an effort to stop the MFM.

'I will be in Dundrum town centre with Cher, the Irish lad off *Celebrity Big Brother*, and Rory McIlroy later today to host a tea-making symposium. Please join us,' the President shared on official social media accounts.

However, members of the MFM have already sabotaged similar events by adding the milk first when no one is looking.

HEALTH AND SCIENCE

93 per cent of people who leave foil on butter tubs are psychopaths

A startling new study has found that a large majority of people who leave the foil on spreadable butter tubs are complete psychopaths who shouldn't be trusted.

The study, carried out by researchers from Harvard University in the United States of America, said people who refuse to just take the foil off, despite the tub already having a lid to keep it fresh, should be referred to the nearest psychiatrist for an assessment, before they do something dangerous to themselves or others.

'These people are completely dangerous and proper precautions should be taken when dealing with them on a daily basis,' the report stated. 'Other warning signs include: resting their free hand palm up on their lap while eating, insisting on putting ketchup in the fridge, and a propensity for eating Marmite, Ritz biscuits or pigs' feet (trotters).'

Of the 93 per cent of people who insisted on leaving the foil on the butter tubs, researchers found that many had severe abandonment issues and were also prone to committing random acts of violence.

'For instance, during one test we put two subjects in a house for a week with one tub of butter. Subject A immediately ripped off the foil when using it,' lead researcher Dr Timothy Jeffries explained. 'When Subject B found the tub had no foil, he refrained from using it and began resenting his housemate over time. Things escalated quite quickly and Subject A ended up stabbing Subject B to within an inch of his life. As it happens, we found this outcome occurred across the board and lost seventeen people to violent deaths during the study.'

If you are concerned about any of the issues raised in this article, please contact your local psychiatrist for an evaluation.

Archaeologists find Ireland's first ever breakfast roll perfectly preserved in Roscommon bog

A portion of Roscommon's renowned bogland was cordoned off by a team of archaeologists after the alarm was raised earlier today by a local who spotted something jutting out of one of the bog's many crevasses.

'Stories have been going round for years that this is where the first breakfast roll was sold, but sure, I'd never thought I'd find it myself,' Roscommon local Eddie Turney told WWN.

The team of archaeologists from Trinity College Dublin was overjoyed to find what they believe is the first ever breakfast roll, still in its original condition thanks to the bog's ability to preserve organic matter.

'We're over the moon. This thing is at least 1,300 years old, so it's a serious, serious find. It will put our group on the map internationally, too,' Dr Erwin Kelly told WWN in a tent close to the original discovery.

While the examination of the breakfast roll is still in the early stages, the experts believe it may have been purchased at a nearby corner shop.

'O'Malley's corner shop has been in the area for a significant period of time, although I'm sure that when this breakfast roll was made the shop was still just a shed, and you had to knock on the door of the O'Malleys' house if you wanted something from the shop,' Dr Kelly revealed.

The group must now explain why the breakfast roll remained uneaten.

'The two dead bodies next to the breakfast roll may provide us with that answer. But legend has it that the breakfast roll was highly sought after once the O'Malley's started making them,' Dr Kelly added.

HEALTH AND SCIENCE

5 signs you have gluten intolerance

Recognising that you have gluten intolerance is not the easiest thing to do as the symptoms can sometimes overlap with other health issues, making it difficult to distinguish what is causing what. In a recent survey, 93 per cent of people who have gluten intolerance have had to diagnose the disease themselves without any professional help. So how do they do it? Here are the five subtle signs to look for:

You've always wanted something to be wrong with you.

Ever since you can remember, you've always wanted some kind of bearable disease to differentiate you from your peers. More than three quarters of people who claim gluten intolerance were found to have common character traits, including a propensity to harass restaurant staff with endless questions about their food despite everything being described on the menu; sniffing every meal before they eat it; and the uncanny ability to annoy everyone they meet, including their own friends and family.

You blame bread for everything.

Have you ever gone on a night out on the town, drank between eight and twelve different types of alcoholic drink and then ended up drunk, eating a kebab, and wakened the next day in an awful way, blaming everything on the kebab bread? Well, you must be gluten intolerant. There is no other explanation for that kind of ailment. Definitely gluten intolerance.

You get tired at night

Do you get tired at night after spending all day awake? Do your legs feel heavy

and fatigued after walking or running? Do you find yourself falling asleep at night, sometimes not waking up for between six and nine hours? If the answer is 'yes', then you're fucked as far as eating bread or pasta goes. Fucked. Give up gluten.

Mood swings

A lot of gluten-intolerant people report 'mood swings' following a family bereavement or tragic accident. This is not normal and is one of the top telltale signs that your body, despite having the benefit of millions of years of human evolution, is intolerant to wheat. So avoid those funeral sandwiches if you want to stay happy. Bread is Satan.

Inflammation

The most common ailment that afflicts those suffering from gluten intolerance is an inflamed ego. Many sufferers believe their needs should be dealt with first when ordering food with a party of people. Speaking only about yourself and your eating habits at every available moment may warrant a quick self-diagnosis online.

NOTE: If you believe you are gluten intolerant, please refrain from seeking any reliable medical advice on the matter and refer to Google search instead.

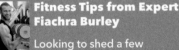

Fitness Tips from Expert Fiachra Burley

Looking to shed a few pounds? Strap a couch or a fridge to yourself when you go out for a jog. Other household items will also work well.

Ireland's most popular sex positions as voted for by WWN readers

10. The puck out

9. Wild Swans at Coole

8. The bucking Kerryman

7. The fiddler's elbow

6. The elongated plough

5. The confession box

4. The 10-pint accidental I didn't mean to put my finger up there, I swear.

3. Peig Sayers' tears

2. The Barrytown Trilogy

1. Missionary

HEALTH AND SCIENCE

EXCLUSIVE

We meet the sickos who won't baptise their child just to get him a place at school

On the surface, the home of Saadiq and Elaine Gurramesh seems like any other household in Ireland. Like you or me, they own chairs, a TV – even toenail clippers, which they forgot to put away even though they knew they had guests arriving.

However, a social faux pas such as this pales into insignificance when compared to the fact that Saadiq and Elaine have hit headlines in their local community after confirming they have no intention of baptising their child just to get him a place in school. Just writing those words fills me with enough anger to go back to their home to slap them both in the face for their selfish idiocy and to place a picture of the Sacred Heart in their hallway.

For their part, the parents of 4-year-old Dharmesh maintain it is their right as non-religious individuals not to baptise their child in the Catholic faith, even though the odds are stacked high against any non-Catholic families in Ireland in terms of access to education. But surely it is our right as a secular nation of lapsed Catholics who don't really believe in the tenets of the faith to be allowed to exclude them for not bowing to immense pressure.

'I'm not Catholic,' Elaine says, as if she's pointing out something important, or as if I'm so supposed to be impressed.

'There are no secular schools near us, and sadly we are far down the list of priorities having only moved here two years ago due to myself and Elaine getting new jobs,' Saadiq said, seemingly unaware of how fucking stupid and selfish he was to get a better-paid job in a new community when his child was two years of age.

To listen to Elaine and Saadiq, it was clear they had no morals or principles. Frankly, they are a danger to their well-fed, healthy and polite child. Despite their horrid ways, which could rightly see a community shun them completely, Saadiq and Elaine have been welcomed with open arms by many people.

'Look, chuck a bit of water on the kid's head and we'll let him in, even though he has a funny name,' explained school chaplain and head of the board of management at Sisters of Mercy Primary School, Fr Michael Mackey.

Fr Mackey explained to the Gurrameshs that such a move would be win-win for all involved as Dharmesh would receive a place in school, and the Catholic church would register the 4-year-old child as a permanent member of the church with no option to renounce his membership once he was an adult.

'He gets to be educated by some amazing state-paid teachers who have to stay in the closet sexually and faith-wise for fear of losing their jobs, and we get to tell the government that about 50,000 thousand kids who are deeply, deeply Catholic start in Junior Infants every year. Kebab's parents are giving out for no good reason, and if you ask me they're weird sickos who obviously don't want the best for their child,' Fr Mackey concluded.

Fr Mackey's sentiments were echoed by a friend of the young family who was so concerned she popped into the house to point out that stubbornly saying 'Ireland's education system is not fit for purpose and does not reflect modern society, and someone should stand up so that this can change' is a bit stupid-sounding.

'Jesus, just give in and baptise the little guy. It's not like it matters. Why are you being so selfish about it?' Emma Hanley, a family friend, asked the couple in response to Elaine's meaningless claim that neither herself or her husband are religious.

'Eh, yeah, and? Neither am I, but it's just the law or whatever. Do it and stop making a show of yourself,' Emma berated Elaine, who at this point was surely beginning to realise the damage she was doing her child.

In an effort to show Dharmesh's parents the true horror of their tyranny and the threat to their son's future prospects, I suggested that they send their son to an Educate Together school with the other lunatic parents who hate their kids.

Bride to have relaxed, chilled-out wedding if it fucking kills her

A Dublin bride-to-be has revealed that the day she walks up the aisle and marries her long-time boyfriend will have an ambience of relaxation and light-hearted fun, even if it requires months of knife-edge tension in a pressure-cooker environment to achieve it.

Bridget Cannavan, 27, will wed Brian Hobson, also 27, on 28 November this year, on a day that will have a chilled-out vibe even

if it takes her every waking moment between now and then to organise it.

Cannavan began preparing for the wedding around this time last year, after her secondary-school squeeze Hobson finally proposed. From the moment she said yes, Cannavan insisted to everyone that she didn't want a huge, elaborate wedding, but instead wanted a day that she describes as 'totally chillaxicated'.

In a bid to achieve 100 per cent total chillaxication on the day, Cannavan began months of preparation in which everything from flowers to cocktail sausages was pored over, in excruciating detail.

'Is turkey and ham more relaxed than roast beef? Someone fucking answer me!' yelled Cannavan to her one-man wedding support team. 'Everyone has to have a great day, everyone has to just kick back and have fun and there has to be no fucking pressure on the day at all, zero pressure whatsoever.

'I know it's only one day, but it's one day that has to be relaxed and chill or else I'm going to fucking hate myself for the rest of my life,' she added.

To help prepare for her calm day of wedded serenity, Cannavan installed a Doomsday Clock in her living room, and is gradually moving the hands closer to midnight to represent the mounting pressure of the preparations.

As of today, the time stands at 11.57.

Chirpy bastard 'never gets hangovers'

'I'm grand, lads, not a bother on me!' Darren Reynolds told friends in his sitting room this morning after what was deemed the most epic Bank Holiday session yet. 'I never get hangovers at all, no matter how much I drink.'

Reynolds, who was out two nights in a row with his clique of friends in Waterford city, was greeted with groans from those he just woken.

'I must have drunk twelve large bottles of Bulmers and about seven JD-and-cokes,' he said, before asking if anyone wanted a fry-up.

Unaware of his annoying and slightly condescending tone, the 26-year-old legend then opened

the sitting room curtains in a bid to 'peel back the day'.

'Aw, for fuck's sake Darren, will you ever fuck off and leave us sleep, you chirpy bastard,' shouted his friend Clarky from the couch. 'Some of us are still skagged outavit from Saturday – lay off with the fucking food talk boy, will ya? M'after eatin' the inside of me jaw, so I'm fine.'

Forcing a perky whistle as he exited the room, the grandson-of-four decided to leave his friends sleep for the moment, but

promised to be back in an hour 'after his 10k run'.

'Go fuck yourself Darren,' everyone thought in unison. 'Go fuck yourself.'

BREAKING NEWS

Fears grow for Dublin teenager who hasn't posted a selfie in over an hour

Concerns have been raised for a Dublin teenager who has failed to upload any selfies to social media for well over an hour.

Cathy McNeil, 16, last posted a picture of herself pouting and holding up two fingers to her Instagram account this morning as she waited for the school bus.

Until today, she had posted selfies every fifteen minutes for two years, never failing to let her followers know exactly where she was and what she was wearing at all times.

Although the teenager has been seen at her school this morning and is in no apparent trouble or stress, an online campaign has been launched by concerned Instagrammers who are keen for McNeil to upload a selfie as soon as she can.

'We're not upset or angry Cathy, we just want you to post a photo of yourself,' said username xxXXxxjustinismybaexxXXxx, in a heartfelt post under the 'WHERESCATHY' hashtag.

This sentiment was echoed by hundreds of Twitter users, who pleaded for anyone with information to come forward. McNeil, currently in fourth year in St Harper's secondary school in Glasnevin, is expected to make a return to regular selfie posting later today after she spends an hour re-touching her eye make-up.

Fitness Tips from Expert Fiachra Burley

Make sure to update your social media accounts regularly. Your friends need to know you were at the gym today.

Increase in number of culchies opting for a bog birth

There has been a 132 per cent increase in the number of culchies opting for a natural bog birth, latest figures have revealed.

The National Registrar for Irish Births has stated that in the last twelve months as many as three thousand culchies have spurned the comfort of the nation's hospitals in

favour of being closer to home and their heritage.

'It's a big thing now with first-time culchie mothers. They have a real aversion to big Dublin hospitals and their notions, and so they are turning to the bog birth,' explained midwife Anna Merchant.

Bog births are similar to home water births. However, in the case of a bog birth, a pregnant mother will retreat into the wilds of Connemara and lie in the bog until labour begins. There are competing schools of thought as to the benefits of bog births, but much like water

births, a bog birth is believed to be more relaxed and comfortable.

As is well known, newborn culchie babies birthed directly into bogland can survive in dense peat for days as they are able to breathe in peat with no adverse effects.

'I just want my child to be born into an environment I'm familiar with, and one he or she will grow to love,' one mother told WWN, as her contractions began and she wedged herself into a peat bog in an effort to get comfortable.

The Year in Stats

30% of married couples in Ireland first met while drunk at 4 a.m., queuing for a kebab.

Local woman has been up since half six this morning

'Hash Wednesday' slowly overtaking Ash Wednesday in popularity

Dungarvan resident Denise Rotchford made sure today to tell every one of her family and friends that she has been up since half six this morning, and there's 'not a bother on her at all'.

Mrs Rotchford first made the bizarre claim at lunchtime, when friend Teresa Ryan yawned and complained about being tired.

'Tired! Sure, I've been up since half six this morning with the kids,' she pointed out, for no particular reason. 'Had the housework done by eleven and even went for a run. I only need a few hours sleep. The father's the same.'

Sources close to the 42-year-old said they do not know why she feels the need to outdo everyone else, or, indeed, why she gets up so damn early in the morning with her children, as they only go to school at 9 a.m.

'I think she's full of shit, to be honest,' said neighbour Maura Nagle, who wishes to remain anonymous. 'If I told her I'd walked up a hill, she'd mention the time she scaled Kilimanjaro on her year out from college.'

Along with her early-bird claims, Mrs Rotchford is also known for her early-morning Facebook posts, containing pictures of the rising sun from her back garden, and various other condescending status updates describing her yoga and running routines.

'If I see one more map from a run app I'll scream,' said friend Tina Murray. 'She makes the rest of us look like lazy hoors.'

The Vatican has finally admitted defeat in their quest to keep Ash Wednesday the most popular observance on the day after Pancake Tuesday, formally known as Shrove Tuesday.

Figures released by the Central Agency for Releasing Figures (CARF) today confirmed that the emerging religious practice called 'Hash Wednesday' is now infinitely more popular than rubbing a bit of ash on your head.

Hash Wednesday involves stockpiling large quantities of hashish and honing your spiritual connection to God by smoking the substance throughout the day.

'This is my first Hash Wednesday, and it's deadly,' confirmed one spiritual individual by the name of Mark Morgan in the chilled-out and relaxed manner typical of Hash Wednesday.

The Vatican, however, has refused to formally incorporate the practice into Catholic religious observance.

'The moment people found out Jesus loved pancakes, they started naming Shrove Tuesday Pancake fucking Tuesday, and now this. Honestly, we give up trying,' confirmed publicist for the Vatican Fr Carlo Fontaggio.

'We tried to get ahead of the game by making the ash out of hash, but then someone told us that putting it on people's heads is not how hash works,' added Fr Fontaggio.

'It's well for some,' says co-worker about everything you do

Office dose Cathal Granning is to continue saying 'it's well for some' as a reply to his co-workers during conversations about things they own or places they visit, after months of him not picking up on the shitty looks he gets when he does so.

So far this week Granning, 38, has said 'it's well for some' after co-workers spoke about things such as upgrading their phone, buying a new car, booking a holiday to Lanzarote, and having a tooth-cleaning procedure done at the dentist.

The staff at McClennon & Roe accountants in Dublin have made no secret of how annoying they find this comment is, but Granning seems to be stuck in some sort of Tourettes-style fit, rendering him unable to say anything else.

'He asked me how my weekend was, I said that I just watched a bit of telly, and he said, "Oh, it's well for some",' said one member of staff we spoke to.

'I think you could tell him that you spent the weekend in A&E after getting the shit kicked out you by a homophobic gang and he'd still say "oh, well for some". He is either a complete moron, trying to wind us up, or he has such a miserable life that he actually envies those who do even the most minor things to treat themselves. I'd believe anything at this stage.'

UPDATE: Granning has received his first punch to the face from a co-worker after noting that it was 'well for some' to get picked for redundancy.

Puppy receives unwanted human for Christmas

In an exclusive interview with WWN, a Labrador puppy has confirmed that it has already tired of the human it received for Christmas, and is wondering if it can go back to living in the dog pound where 'there's a bit of craic'.

The three-month-old Lab was adopted by a single Waterford woman in her mid-thirties, as an 'early Christmas present to herself'.

Although the puppy, who answers to the name Jack, was initially thrilled to receive a human for Christmas, this excitement soon wore off when he realised the effort needed to cope with a fully-grown woman who does nothing but post pictures of herself with her dog on Facebook in a bid to fool everyone into thinking that she's totally all right with being the only one of her friends who is still single.

'I thought it would be great to get a human for Christmas but, Jesus Christ, it's a lot of work,' said Jack, taking a well-earned lick of his balls.

'But the constant posing for pictures, having an iPhone in your face all the time ... it's way more hassle than I thought it would be. Honestly, send me back to the dog shelter where I don't have to put up with this woman trying to balance a Santa hat on my head while lining up a shot of the TV and a wine glass in the background, for an Instagram post titled "Perfect night in with my man LOL".'

Puppies across the country have been advised to think long and hard about whether or not they want a human this Christmas, as humans are unfortunately for life, not just for Christmas Day.

A County Kilkenny man purchased two trays of blackberries and a fruit salad mix in his local shop today for him to throw out next week.

Thomas Casey spent €7.49 for the packaged fruit as part of a new health plan he came up with at the fruit and veg aisle, which he believes will reverse years of unhealthy eating, drinking and smoking.

'I'll make sure to push it right to the back of my fridge,' he explained, knowing full well he'll forget about the perishable food products in a

Man purchases fruit for himself to throw out next week

matter of seconds. 'It should have rotted enough by next week for me to just throw it into the bin, like that watermelon I bought three weeks ago.'

On 29 October, the 44-year-old bought a whole watermelon as part of a health kick he lost interest in after a few days.

'I cut it up into slices and then wrapped the pieces in cling film as if I was actually going to eat them at some stage,' he admitted. 'Who was I fooling, eh? You can't just refrigerate fruit and expect to come back to it later on. I'll never learn.'

So far this year, Casey has spent over €300 on various fruit items he has subsequently never consumed.

'The initial feeling I get when I buy the fruit overrides the haunting guilt of throwing it out,' he concluded.

BREAKING NEWS

Parents on weekend away from the kids contemplate never going back

David and Marian Dempsey, a married couple from Louth, were said to be locked in intense conversation while on a weekend trip to Kerry.

The couple, parents to three young children, are believed to be giving strong consideration to never going back, instead preferring to seek out a new life.

While enjoying the luxurious surroundings of a 4-star hotel and spa resort it is alleged Marian hit upon the idea of ripping up her identity and removing all traces of her existence.

'It was probably just after I had my first massage I thought, "Wouldn't it be great if I didn't have to go back". I don't want

people thinking I'm a monster but, like, just imagine,' Marian exclusively told WWN.

'They'd be grand with Marian's sister, sure. We have an awful habit of telling the kids what to do and that, so it's probably best if we try to move away to somewhere like the Caribbean,' added husband David.

'The kids, they're not little shits or anything, but you sort of, occasionally, wish you never had them and could just enjoy life, ya know?' speculated Marian.

It is believed that the Dempseys are part of the 100 per cent of parents who give consideration to 'pulling a legger' on their children.

The Year in Stats

Longford hasn't come up in conversation since 22 October 1955.

Couple spend 12 hours browsing Netflix without picking a movie

A Waterford couple who were looking forward to nothing more than a laze on the couch while watching a movie on Netflix have found themselves caught in an endless spiral of browsing and indecision.

'No, you fucking said you wanted to watch a romantic comedy and we spent thirty minutes looking for

one, but now you're "okay" with an action movie, fuck's sake like,' Ciara Bellion screamed at her boyfriend of two years, Martin Reilly, as the difficulty of simply picking a movie revealed itself.

Initially, several movie titles were put on a 'maybe/back-up' list in the event of the couple's failure to find something better. However, due to the list being made in Ciara and Martin's heads, it was soon forgotten, forcing the search to start over again.

'Ah, I was well in the mood for *When Harry Met Sally* but when we typed it in they suggested *Mona Lisa Smile*. If I wanted *Mona Lisa Smile* I would have typed *Mona*

fucking Lisa Smile into the search yoke,' Martin explained to WWN, highlighting his frustration with the fact that Netflix has fuck-all decent movies on the popular streaming service.

Four hours into their search for a nice light movie that would help them both wind down after a long day of work, Ciara and Martin began to rule out movies longer than ninety minutes on account of the fact it was 11.30 p.m.

'We had decided on *Pain and Gain*, you know, it has The Rock, like, it's obviously gonna be class, but the fuckin' thing is over two hours long,' Ciara lamented while flicking between genres on the Netflix interface.

With the time now approaching 3 a.m., the irritable couple are no closer to finding the right movie and may be left with no alternative but to start *Breaking Bad* from the beginning again.

Confusion continues to be served on a daily basis as one rural man refuses to accept that dinner is the meal eaten at the end of the day, and not from 1 p.m. to 2 p.m.

Cathal Moran, originally from Ballybay, but a Dublin resident for the last four years, continues to refer to lunchtime as dinnertime, and dinnertime as teatime.

This rift in the meal-time continuum has led to several instances when Moran has missed out on meeting people or attending important appointments, simply by not clarifying what he means when he says, 'I'll see you at dinner time.'

Friends and co-workers have expressed annoyance at the 37-year-old's refusal to accept the difference between 'dinner

Culchie to continue having 'dinner and tea' instead of 'lunch and dinner'

and tea' and 'lunch and dinner,' adding that Moran has continued to add further caveats to his already stupid system.

'If he eats a big meal at 1 p.m. and another at 6 p.m., he calls it

"having two dinners",' said one co-worker we talked to.

'And if he only eats a sandwich at lunchtime, he's annoyed because he had "no dinner". You have your dinner in the evening, you thick fuck. Jesus Christ, it's annoying.'

Moran steadfastly refuses to call any meal 'supper', as he believes that supper is 'something that Protestants eat'.

ROSE OF TRALEE

ASK IRELAND: **Are we ready for a male Rose Of Tralee?**

The annual Rose Of Tralee Festival is the only remaining female-centric event in Ireland, following the cancellation of both the Calor Housewife of the Year competition and the religious free-for-all known as The Nunger Games.

But there are those that claim that the rot has started to set in to the ROT, and that the glitzy gala needs to move with the times by including contestants from other genders. Our opinion? Shit, don't ask us – ASK IRELAND:

'A male Rose Of Tralee? What next? A woman guard? Cop yourself on!'

Sean McAggert, 96

'I think that anybody should be allowed to enter anything. Gender is a construct that we enforce to keep society from ever feeling as one. We need to understand that we're all just … ah shite, she wasn't listening. Sorry, I was just trying to sound clever so I could have a chance with that fine thing over there, but she's paying no attention. What's the question again?'

Michael Ring, 27

'Great. That's all I need. More sharks in the fucking tank.'

Sinead Harrington, Kerry Rose, 21

'This is the kind of shit I warned everyone about back in 1995. You vote yes for divorce in Ireland, and it's just the start of it. We haven't started eating babies yet, but this is just another step closer!'

Anne-Sarah McCelennan, 39

'Yes.'

Paul Galvin, 36

'If they can recite a poem about a holiday they took with their grandmother the year before she passed away from throat cancer, then they're all right by me.'

Ian Marron, 45

'Just so I'm clear … are you talking about real men? Or transgender men? Not that transgender men aren't real men, I mean, eh … I mean like people who were born men. Or are you talking about men who were born as women but have transitioned back to being men? Not that they weren't men all along, they were just women who identified as men but now they're men who – oh crap, I think I'm having a stroke, get help please.'

Helen Gallagher, 34

'Who gives a fuck.'

Anon

Most controversial Rose Of Tralee moments

The Rose of Tralee is Ireland's most treasured competition. It appraises a woman's various qualities as she stands there in a nice dress, but the historic event hasn't been without its controversies. Ahead of the start of this year's Rose of Tralee, we bring you the 10 most controversial moments in its storied history:

10. The controversial decision to award balaclava-wearing IRA Rose Deirdre McDonald the crown in 1994 did not go down well with the public as they were angered that her balaclava was not knitted by her granny, but was in fact bought in Carrolls Gift Shop. Shocking.

9. Who can forget the moment Alaskan Rose Ann Cummings' bear-taming routine went awry on stage. We all watched, engrossed by the horror, as the loose bear named John Joe mauled original Rose of Tralee host Kevin Hilton to death. A tragedy? Yes. A ratings hit? Most definitely.

8. 1999 Carlow Rose Roisin Hennigan forgot the fifth decade of the Rosary live on air, an error that ultimately cost her the crown. Devastating. #WeAllRememberWhereWeWereWhenRoisinHenniganForgotThe5thDecadeOfTheRosaryOnTheRoseOfTralee

7. 1987 Rose of Tralee winner Ciara Healy lifted a car above her head for five minutes as her special talent. Truly memorable and her achievement provided scientists with conclusive proof that women can be strong AND beautiful.

6. It was 'awkward central' when Ryan Tubridy's mike picked up the experienced host saying 'What the fuck am I doing here?' under his breath several times throughout the first night of the competition. Viewers were further offended when Tubridy asked Dublin Rose Abigail O'Neill if she loved her Mammy and Daddy. Of course she did, she's not a fucking monster.

5. Frank Sinatra singing live at the 1967 Rose of Tralee. Stardust was sprinkled over the exalted Kerry venue and rumours that Ol' Blue Eyes took all Roses back to his hotel room persist to this day.

4. Guest host Jay Leno caused a stir with an off-colour Famine joke during his 2004 hosting stint and was subsequently beaten to a bloody pulp live on stage by a gang of Healy-Raes.

3. US President Bill Clinton took to the Rose of Tralee stage to play a two-hour sax solo in 1997. Amazing. Some will be surprised this didn't take the top slot.

2. 1971 saw a Dublin Rose win for the first time, but Mary Murray was disqualified after it was discovered she was a Protestant. Dishonest.

1. New York Rose and performance artist Rosemary Cullen took heroin on stage to highlight substance abuse problems in Ireland in the 80s. She overdosed. The memories.

ROSE OF TRALEE

Investigation into Rose Of Tralee finds contestants are 30 per cent more lovely than previously estimated

An investigation which has shaken the Rose of Tralee to its very core has discovered that the contestants are 30 per cent more lovely than previously estimated, resulting in widespread outrage among the Rose of Tralee-loving public.

'We apologise profusely for our error in estimating just how fine these fine young things are,' ashen-faced Rose of Tralee organiser Barra Boland explained to international media. 'We at no point set out to deliberately obscure the level of loveliness from the public. It is just that, as a modern pageant celebrating Irish women, we have moved with the times and upgraded our method of calculation and now use cutting-edge technology.'

Boland explained that the competition had previously used local Tralee-based grandmothers as a barometer for gauging contestants' loveliness up until 2013, but have now switched to a system developed by a scientist at MIT in America.

Smiling grannies who would say variations of the phrase 'awk, look at her, she's gorgeous. I bet she's lovely to her mother' have now given way to Roses being subjected to weeks worth of testing to calculate their loveliness. With the latest available data, it is very clear that Roses are some 30 per cent more lovely than previously thought, which will have ramifications for the competition going forward.

'Well, we'll make more money out of stupid Americans for a start,' local Tralee businessman Ciaran Colgan told WWN.

However, not everyone is happy with the news.

'I dunno, I feel like something sinister is going on. Why didn't they tell us they were that bit more comely? Do they think we can't handle the truth,' shared Fiachra Tolan, an 86-year-old bachelor from Kerry who is still holding out hope of finding Mrs Right.

What the Roses did next

1. The first ever winner of the Rose of Tralee campaign Roisin Doherty is fondly remembered, and the Rose all Roses aspire to emulate. However, the competition in its first year little resembles the modern and forward-thinking contest we know and love today. Due to rules governing the winner of the competition, Roisin was required to have nineteen children or risk having her crown taken away from her. Thankfully, that was avoided as Roisin immediately married her escort (another requirement) and dedicated her life to having children non-stop.

2. The 1979 Carlow Rose Olwyn McGettigan is a Rose the organisers would probably hope people have forgotten about, but such was the mark that McGettigan made in her post-Rose of Tralee career that is nigh impossible. McGettigan had stated that once the competition was over she would be heading to the Congo to carry out missionary work. When RTÉ travelled to the Congo a year later to film a documentary about McGettigan's work, they were shocked to find she was the barbaric leader of a child militia.

3. Following a rule change in 1996 after Sharon Ní Bheoláin won the Rose of Tralee for an eighth year in a row, organisers insisted only first-time Roses would be allowed to take part in the competition; enter stage right the Calcutta Rose Mother Teresa. The then 86-year-old wowed judges with her ability to be so holy, and secured the crown in spectacular fashion with her special talent of denying poor children food and necessary medical attention. Mother Teresa would die the following year, but she has succeeded where all other Roses have failed by being made a saint by Pope Francis.

4. In an effort to shore up the Irish-American vote for her husband, Hillary Clinton entered the 1990 Rose of Tralee as the Arkansas Rose, while her husband went on to win the US presidential election. Next to nothing has been heard about his wife since.

ROSE OF TRALEE

Woman's quirkiness cemented with new fringe

Student of the arts Emma Holden has today cemented her inner quirkiness with a brand new fringe, aptly named a 'front bang', which currently sits two inches above her brow.

The 26-year-old launched her new look on Facebook, updating her account with a post-cut profile picture, and a statement, that reads 'finally got it done'.

It is understood Ms Holden spent hours debating the cropped style with family and friends, several of whom had already made the leap.

'My friend Deirdre said that since she got hers done all the art crowd in town have started speaking to her and asking her to cool events with free wine. She even got an invite to a Japanese anime night at the old cinema,' Holden told WWN.

'The front bang is very 1970s New York and it is deffo the hairstyle for me,' she added.

Since opting for her new look, the granddaughter-of-four said she regularly finds herself reading up on French literature, and insists that she will probably fall for a man with the same interests.

'My next boyfriend will probably be a creative type who'll get on brilliantly with my large clique of friends,' she imagined, with her mind. 'I like the name Tony, but I'm not all that fussy really, a Paul or a Clive will do.'

'You can wash my car when you're done,' jests hilarious neighbour

For the hundredth time, the avenues of a small Wicklow suburb have rung loud with laughter as local man Sean Cahill cracked his amazingly hilarious 'you can wash my car when you're done' joke to one of his neighbours.

Cahill, a grown man, trots out the classic line every time he sees one of his neighbours washing their car, usually once a week.

Despite not knowing his neighbours by name, Cahill still thinks he's on good enough terms with everyone to walk up to them as they're washing their car and suggest in a jovial manner that they clean his when they're done.

This amazing lark is not limited to car washing, it also applies to car hoovering, lawn mowing, window washing and gutter clearing, giving Cahill plenty of opportunities to show the residents of Hazelbrook Drive just how much of a gas character he really is.

'You should see the look on their faces when I say "you can clean mine when you're finished",' said Cahill, doubled over with laughter.

'I say "you can clean mine when you're finished" and they just give me a face as if to say "ha ha, nice one". I'm not doing it justice here, you'd really have to see it to get the full glory of it.'

Cahill's neighbours were unavailable for comment, because they hate him.

Toddler morphs into dickhead the second he enters restaurant

A County Waterford couple who decided to go for a meal with their two-year-old son were left dumbfounded today after he instantaneously 'morphed into a dickhead' just seconds after sitting down in the restaurant.

Jason Purcell reluctantly sat at the table and then just began crying for

no reason whatsoever despite his parents' best efforts to appease him with promises of ice cream and sprinkles, an order immediately given to waiting staff.

'For the love of God, can someone get us crayons, paper, anything to shut this little bollox up?' dad David begged, frantically

looking around the restaurant for anything or anyone to help. 'Where's an angry-looking old man when you need one?'

The toddler, who learned at an early stage that Mammy and Daddy never threaten him in public, bellowed uncontrollably, knowing his treat was on its way.

'Here ya go now,' said the child's mother as the waiter delivered the bowl, before whispering into Jason's ear. 'One more fucking word out of you and I swear to God, you won't be able to sit down for a week.'

Irish junior doctor doesn't mind working for a week straight without any sleep

The predicament that junior doctors working within the HSE find themselves in doesn't bother them at all, one junior doctor has told WWN.

Speaking to WWN with an intravenous coffee drip attached to her veins, Ciara Rafferty, a doctor in St Vincent's Hospital, said working a full week with close to no sleep is in fact 'grand'.

'Look, honestly, it's fine. Seeing a huge number of Irish medical professionals move abroad in order to achieve more than four hours of sleep a week is, frankly, crybaby stuff, like. Get over yourself, thinking you're entitled to some quality of life,' Rafferty told WWN in before she dozed off while standing upright.

Colleagues of Rafferty's echoed her sentiments, admitting that working upwards of twenty-four hours with little time for food or rest is actually fine, and they even went as far as to confirm that the government shouldn't be bothered trying to fix systemic failures within the HSE.

'Look me in the eye and tell me that junior doctors pushed to the limits in an underfunded, atrociously

run HSE doesn't fill you with confidence,' Rafferty added, but try as we might to catch her eye, she had fallen asleep again.

Junior doctors in Ireland haven't 'got a leg to stand on' when it comes to complaints about working conditions, according to the government, who cite the fact the European Court of Justice failed to fine them for being in breach of the Working Time Directive as evidence that it's like Disneyland out there for young doctors.

'Ah no, honestly, they're having a lovely time,' confirmed government spokesman Declan Nevison.

'While my colleagues and I appreciate the tireless concern the public has shown for us and our

patients, it's grand. I actually like working non-stop with no sleep. Some of the hallucinations you have from being so sleep deprived are pretty trippy,' Rafferty added, in an attempt to explain away a dream she thought she had about giving someone you know the wrong dosage.

BREAKING NEWS

Weather warning in place after cold breeze fatally cuts Dublin man in two

Gardaí and emergency services have today issued a severe weather warning after a Dublin cyclist was pronounced dead on Eden Quay after being cut in two by what can only be described as a 'fatal breeze'.

Traffic was brought to a standstill after motorists stopped to help the young man, who is believed to have bled to death after being ripped from the groin up through the torso, severing his entire body into two equal pieces.

'Both sides of him just seemed to flop down to the left and right of his bicycle,' motorist and eyewitness Terrence Williams recalled. 'People were screaming in shock, so I stopped to see if I could help, but he was already dead by the time he hit the ground.'

It is understood the man was wearing nothing but a pair of shorts and a T-shirt at the time of his death, forcing Gardaí to issue a nationwide weather warning.

'We would ask people travelling by bike or by foot to wrap up well, and not be fooled by the sun into thinking it's warm out there,' Garda Commissioner Nóirín O'Sullivan stated. 'There's a breeze in it that would cut you in two, so be safe.'

The unnamed man is the fourth Irish person this year to be cut in two by cold north-westerly winds.

Waterford mother nicknames her slow descent into alcoholism 'wine o'clock'

Waterford mother Grainne Filan has given her slow descent into alcoholism the humorous and wry nickname 'wine o'clock', WWN has learned.

The 49-year-old mother of three has referred privately to her consistent and worrisome consumption of both red and white wines with the words 'wine o'clock', followed by a short but loud giggle, much to the decreasing amusement of those closest to her.

Initially 'wine o'clock' struck once every couple of weeks in the company of friends or with Grainne's husband Stephen. However, Grainne now observes the specific time of day by herself, with increasingly large numbers of 'just the one glass'.

Sources close to Grainne confirm that in recent years the official commencement of 'wine o'clock' has been brought forward from 9 p.m. to as early as 5 p.m.

Using a clever method to obscure the fact that she regularly feels the need to stock up on alcohol, insurance broker Grainne, mother of Niall (19), Mairead (15), and Orlaigh (12), pretends to be in constant need of food from the local shop despite ample supplies already present in her presses and fridge.

'Just need more mushrooms – we never have enough of them, do we?' Grainne commented early yesterday evening on her way to purchase five bottles of wine, three of which she hid from view at the back of the hot press.

Best locations for a piss-up or a session as voted for by WWN readers

5. Behind any Lidl or corner shop. Few cans. Can't beat it.

4. Any old abandoned and creepy-looking gaff. The ambience is second to none.

3. Mountjoy Prison. Several prisoners run craft breweries from their prison cells.

2. Any christening. They always have the best coke.

1. Dáil bar. No one knows how to rack up a bar tab like those revellers.

The mother-of-three's slow descent into alcoholism is set to gather pace with the days getting shorter, as the darker evenings bring 'wine o'clock' forward by an hour.

Perfect fucking family insists on leaving curtains open at night for everyone to see

A County Kilkenny family of five has come under fire from local residents this week for constantly leaving their curtains open at night, allowing everyone to see into their perfect fucking lives.

Karl and Tina Tobin, who bought their five-bedroom home in Elm Pines last year, are accused of 'flaunting' their functional family to the whole street and carrying on like they don't even know they're being watched.

'They make me sick,' neighbour Tommy O'Donoghue told WWN this evening. 'It's the first house you see coming into the estate and

you can see straight in their sitting room window at night because they leave the curtains open for everyone to see.'

The Elm Pines Residents' Association claims the Tobins are

constantly rubbing everyone's noses in it with their impeccable way of living.

'The whole family always seem to be engaging and in good humour,' chairman Ted Baker explained. 'They were even playing Ludo one time when I passed. Fucking Ludo! Who even plays that any more? I'd swear it's all put on for show.'

'The whole thing is perverted, if you ask me,' claimed another neighbour, who believes that people who leave their curtains open are actually hiding something. 'The husband's eyes are very close together too. I just get that feeling from him, you know?'

When asked, the Tobin family refused to comment on the unusual practice, instead advising everyone to 'mind their own business'.

'There's a guilty statement if ever I heard one,' said long-time Elm Pines resident Paddy Hackett. 'The cracks are slowly beginning to show now.'

Inspirational Quote of the Year

'Sing like no one is listening. Love like you've never been hurt. Dance like nobody is watching. Put inspirational quotes up on Facebook to appear deep.'

The Year in Stats

43% of the nation is still calling Snickers bars Marathon bars.

Top 5 Masses of 2016

5. Fr Peter Drury. Dundrum, Dublin. 11.30 a.m., Sunday 21 March.

4. Fr Willie Temple. Carrick-on-Suir, Tipperary. Biddy Eames Funeral Mass, Tuesday 3 May.

3. Pope Francis. Surprise Mass, Donnybrook Church, Dublin. 6.30 p.m., Thursday 8 September.

2. Fr Séan Makalaki Umbet. Belmullet, Mayo. Wedding Mass of Gerry Mullen, Ciara Cassidy, Lorna Hegarty, Laura Cassin, Helen Holding and Caoimhe O'Connor, Saturday 29 October.

1. Fr Bruce Springsteen, specially ordained for the occasion, Croke Park, Dublin. Friday 27 May.

Waterford woman hospitalised after jumping to conclusion

A local Waterford woman is believed to be seriously injured after jumping to conclusions, WWN has learned.

Sheena O'Rahily, a 34-year-old mother of two, suffered the injuries while observing heavy pedestrian traffic outside the house of a neighbour early yesterday morning.

O'Rahily, who often jumps to conclusions without suffering any damage, caught sight of a number of men entering the house across the road, and surmised that its occupant Deirdre Kelly, a married woman, must be having affairs.

'Shortly after 11 a.m., when a workman, believed to be installing a new Sky box, was seen entering a neighbour's house Mrs O'Rahily made a huge leap, concluding that her neighbour was conducting affairs in full view of the street. The conclusion reached involved jumping a great distance and thus shattered a number of Mrs O'Rahily's bones,' Dr Edmund Price shared with reporters outside Waterford Regional Hospital.

O'Rahily is expected to make a full recovery, but will spend several months in hospital.

Doctors fear the woman's absence from her home as she recovers could spark a jumping to conclusions epidemic amongst her own neighbours with many presuming O'Rahily has run off with the postman.

'Daredevil busybodies such as Mrs O'Rahily rarely think of the consequences or the risk of injury and we'd caution others to learn from her mistakes,' added Dr Price.

The number of people hospitalised so far this year for jumping to conclusions has reached over one thousand, with doctors continuing to warn people to resist the urge to jump with little or no evidence to back up their opinions or claims, with a special warning issued to people automatically presuming their new 'Middle Eastern-looking' neighbours are in league with ISIS.

'It's a disgrace I have to travel home from Thailand every month, just to sign on'

Today we speak to Irishman Daniel Casey on the trials and tribulations of having to travel home every month to sign on to our 'outdated' social welfare system.

Speaking to us exclusively on the airport bus into Dublin town, Casey gave us some insight into his monthly trek and what it entails.

'I left Bangkok this time yesterday evening,' he began, clearly exhausted from the long-haul flight. 'I swear, if I see the film *Birdman* on that plane again, I'll murder someone.'

Originally from Ballybrack in the south of the county, it didn't take Casey very long to get down to the brass tacks of it all.

'Twenty hours each way for the sake of a miserable €800 a month is a fucking joke, if you ask me,' Daniel barked, somehow finding the energy needed for such a heartfelt statement. 'Only for the few nixers in the Irish bar I work at, I wouldn't be able to afford the flights at all.'

Spending up to €400 a month on travel expenses, even with frequent-flier miles, the barman called on the Minister for Social Protection to 'relax' the department's strict monthly signing-on regime, calling it old fashioned and not up to the lifestyle of the average twenty-first-century dole claimant.

'It's a disgrace that an Irishman, born and bred here, has to travel all this way, just to sign on,' he said. 'That extra few pound I spend every month could go on more important things, like a housekeeper for the gaff. It's one law for Joan Burton and her cronies and one law for us. I just don't see myself doing this for another seven years, you know?'

Clearly upset, tired and emotional, Casey finally stood up to say his goodbyes, making one last point before he left.

'It's time this government started looking after its own people abroad, instead of minding those from abroad like their own people.'

Entire bus treated to dance music pulsating from dickhead's earphones

Dublin bus commuters found themselves in the enviable position of being offered an exclusive music performance via the earphones of fellow commuter and apparent dickhead, 18-year-old Dean Hanley.

Taking to the back of the top deck on the 15b bus, Hanley immediately began a stirring performance by sticking a dance song on his phone and playing it far too loudly through his earphones, fully aware that he was probably ruining the bus journey for a number of his fellow passengers.

Nodding his head back and forth aggressively, Hanley risked giving himself self-imposed whiplash as well as obliterating his eardrums thanks to his state-of-the-art Beats headphones, which since being acquired by Apple have yet to install vital dickhead-repellent technology.

'I wouldn't mind, to be honest, only for the fact it's Calvin-fucking-Harris he's playing,' explained disgruntled commuter Adrian Cummings, who felt like he was right next to a giant nightclub sound system despite being some nine rows in front of Hanley.

Coming in at a modest 130 decibels, the latest Harris dancefloor hit 'Baggy Fanny' has only smashed two windows on the top deck so far, but with Hanley not getting off until he's in the city centre, there is every chance the high volume could destroy the entire bus.

'Ah, God be with the days when you'd bring your vinyl player on the bus into town. A bit of Dickie Rock would have the bus in convulsions,' remarked pensioner

Ailbhe Doherty, who confirmed she was just about ready to 'fucking end that young fella' if his performance carried on much longer.

NASA drafted in to help Waterford mother find where all the time goes

A crack team of NASA scientists has today been enlisted by the Irish government to help Waterford mother, Theresa Hartigan, finally get to the bottom of where all the time goes.

The elusive nature of time has haunted the 62-year-old mother of seventeen for much of her adult life, which has seen her devoting large chunks of conversations to speculating as to its whereabouts.

'This has been going on for years,' Theresa told WWN shortly after learning the government had appealed to NASA for help. 'One minute I'm chatting away to someone, and the next thing I'm an hour or two in the future. I'd love to know where it all goes.

'Jesus! It's after happening again! I have to go make the dinner,' she added, rushing back into her home.

NASA scientists are expected to run countless tests and experiments on Theresa when they jet into Waterford later this week.

'We will check for a propensity to prattle on incessantly and idly gossip and also test for the presence of dithering. We feel this may be at the root of the rip in Theresa's space-time continuum,' head of the NASA research team, Kent Bent, told WWN.

487 deaths result from that thing Ireland doesn't talk about

According to the latest available figures from the Central Statistics Office a total of 487 people died in 2013 as a result of that thing Ireland doesn't talk about.

The deaths continue a trend that started in 2007 and shows that the numbers of people dying from

that thing we don't talk about are increasing.

While a number of factors have been attributed to the rise, concerns have been raised about the prevalence of that thing among the youth of Ireland.

'It's troubling, and I want with every fibre in my body for something to be done about it, but look if it's all right, I'd prefer you didn't bring it up at all,' Suzanne O'Gorran, spokesperson for the Irish Commission On Things We Don't Talk About told WWN.

The government also stressed its reluctance to talk about the thing, but is said to be relieved that

the statistics have come close to levelling off.

'That is a relief as we can now look into how to continue to do nothing about it. If we get this right, we could even cut funding a bit,' a government spokesperson shared with WWN. The government confirmed it was available to talk about the recovery, road safety campaigns and sugar tax.

Many members of the public have admitted to being aware of someone they know doing that thing, but owing to the troubling nature of talking openly about something in Ireland, they remain reluctant to speak.

BREAKING NEWS

Some bollocks in tractor to ruin every motorist's day today

An absolute bollocks in a tractor has confirmed that he will set out around lunchtime to purposely annoy as many road users as humanly possible today.

Peadar Murphy, who has worked in the farming industry since the age of ten, first set about loading his trailer with twenty large bales of straw for the planned four-hour journey ahead.

'Best double stack them to scare the shit out of people behind,' said the 33-year-old. 'People are less likely to overtake if they think the load is about to topple over on them.'

Mr Murphy admitted to WWN that the bales were 'only there for show', and he isn't actually bringing them anywhere in particular.

'Summer is fairly quiet on the farm so I just go for spins during the day with the tractor and load,' he explained. 'Busy primary and secondary roads are the best craic. Sometimes me and the other farmers have a competition to see how many cars we can hold up behind us.

'One time I had a line of forty-three cars on the Limerick to Cahir main road,' he added,

laughing maniacally into his hand. 'Some horns were blowing that day!'

With a top speed of twenty miles an hour, the father of fourteen's tractor has got him into numerous road-rage incidents over the years.

'I remember some lad in a Honda Civic got sick of being stuck behind me and tried to pass me on this narrow road outside Clonmel,' he recalled. 'He kept up beside me beeping like a lunatic. Sure, I just started waving at him all nice, like he was saying hello or something. Unfortunately, he didn't see the articulated truck coming towards him and ploughed into the thing. That's what he got for not being patient.'

At any one time, there are an estimated three thousand cunts in tractors driving aimlessly on Irish roads in a bid to ruin just about everyone's day.

ELECTRIC PICNIC

10 stunning Electric Picnic facts

Now Ireland's largest music and arts festival, Electric Picnic has soared in popularity from its humble beginnings in 1973. Here are ten facts you proably don't know about the hoo-hally in Stradbally.

1) The first EP was powered by a cable running from Wicklow.

With electricity unavailable in Laois until the mid-nineties, revellers heading to the first EP in 1973 had their experience powered by a cable that was sneakily run across two counties and hooked up to some lad's house in Bray. The unwitting householder received a bill of nearly 8 old pounds, approximately €135,000!

2) Up until the 1980s, there were only ninety-seven artisan food stalls at EP.

It took until 1984 for the artisan food section of EP to really come into its own. Until then, there were less than a hundred organic food stalls! In 1979, they didn't even have venison hotdogs! Mental!

3) The Rolling Stones were kept off the 1989 bill by The Hothouse Flowers.

Mick & co. were forced to take their gyrations and pouts elsewhere, in favour of a three-hour set by the HHF boys.

4) Legendary EP slasher 'Jimmy Blades' claimed his first victim in 1991.

Every camper in EP knows the story of Jimmy Blades, the seemingly supernatural serial killer who picks off teenagers, one by one every year, and returns from the grave whenever someone gets lucky enough to 'kill' him. But did you know Jimmy Blades first showed up in 1991, during a Planxty set? There's a reason they only have one lad on bodhrán these days, you know.

5) The owner of Slane is barred.

Lord Henry Mountcharles is banned for life from attending EP, after a disruptive incident in 1996 when he took to the stage, raging about 'inferior acoustics' that didn't hold a candle to the 'natural amphitheatre' at Slane.

6) We met your ma there one year.

Crazy night. Ask her about us.

7) It keeps going all year.

Think EP stops on the Monday when you pack up and go home? That's what they want you to think. In reality, the party keeps going the entire year round, with only a select few ravers proving hardcore enough to last the whole 365-day session. You didn't think they took down all that staging and put it back up again every year, did you?

8) The Oxegen stage only lasted a day.

In a bid to appease people who only went to EP because Oxegen had folded, a special section of the grounds was dedicated to recreating the Oxegen experience – shit bands, €9 hotdogs, burning tents and dozens of fights later, the stage was shut down after twelve hours and never appeared again.

9) Kids love EP.

Ask any kid under eight if they'd rather go to Disneyland or Electric Picnic, and they'll say EP every time. More people should bring their children to Electric Picnic. It's the perfect environment for them. Are your kids familiar with drug use, casual sex and excessive alcohol consumption? No? Well, they have to learn sometime.

10) EP 2019 is already sold out.

Tickets for EP 2020, 2021 and 2022 are on sale now!

11 things everyone should do at Electric Picnic

1. Plant a tree.

2. Adopt an endangered rhino. There won't be any rhinos on site obviously. Just keep an eye out for a girl with dreadlocks weeping onto a picture of a newborn rhino – she'll sign you up to adopt a rhino after a brief meditation session.

3. Giving birth on the main stage in the middle of LCD Soundsystem's gig. Everyone who's anybody is doing it – it'd be a shame for you to miss out on the cool points.

4. Lead a funeral procession for a recently departed worm. Every living creature deserves a proper burial, followed by a Month's Mind.

5. Pass out while in a portaloo because of the deadly smell.

6. Practise saying 'Oh my God, you just had to be there'. It'd be a wasted trip to a muddy field in Laois if, upon your return to normal life, you couldn't passively aggressively imply that you had a great time and anyone who didn't go is about as cool as Pat Kenny.

7. Get a tattoo you can pretend not to regret for the rest of your life. WWN recommends the Unicorn Shitting Out a Leprechaun with the word 'hope' written above it.

8. Wake up in the wrong tent. It'll be a story for life, which ironically enough is the sentence you'll get after Gardaí hear the screams of the children in the family-friendly camping area after you fall into their tent.

9. Go see a band so unknown they've yet to form. While everyone has their favourite – 'Oh my God, you haven't heard of [insert shit name of shit band here]?' – go one step further and make sure you see a band that is so cool and underground that it hasn't even formed yet. What's more hipster than that?

10. Fall in love with someone called Sunflower. To be fair, her name is likely Ciara and she's just trying to shed society's conventions in the liberating surroundings of Laois, but you haven't lived until you've locked your locked eyes with some fully grown eejit with a face covered in face paint.

11. Declare your love for U2. Watch as the hipster population of Electric Picnic descend into a violent meltdown, which ruins their entire weekend. For a bonus, mention how you actually think Bono is sound too.

ELECTRIC PICNIC

BREAKING NEWS

Gardaí arrest twelve after fight over who heard of Arcade Fire first breaks out amongst hipsters

There were violent scenes at the Stradbally estate this morning as riot police were drafted in to break up a brawl between rival hipster gangs.

The source of the dispute arose when two hipsters were queuing by a food truck, which sold ethically sourced falafel, and one of the men alleged he had heard of Arcade Fire before the release of their debut album, *Funeral*.

Not wanting to be outdone, the second hipster confessed to hearing Arcade Fire singer Win Butler's first ever breath, which the Canadian native took shortly after birth.

'All I heard was a shout of "no, I heard of them first" and then two lads were pulling the man buns off each other. There was blood everywhere,' an eyewitness confirmed.

Gardaí arrested twelve hipsters, but the barbaric fight was not without its victims.

'Hipsters are famously empty individuals who, due to an absence of genuinely compelling and engaging personality traits, attempt to deflect from such shortcomings through trying to appear as cool as possible,' explained noted hipster whisperer Dr Paul Bremnor.

'If challenged on any part of their cool identity they will lash out, as evidenced by the bloody scenes today which claimed the lives of 8 Gardaí, 4 hipsters and thankfully all members of The Coronas as well as leading to 12 arrests,' Dr Bremnor added.

4 ways to improve your festival Portaloo experience

Festivals are among the greatest weekends one can have in a muddy field for €200 a head, but they do come with their drawbacks. Chief among them are Portaloos, which are quick to turn into something more terrifying than the image of Daniel O'Donnell having sex. WWN has uncovered four essential ways the horrid trip to the Portaloos can be improved:

1. Plan ahead.

If you're serious about avoiding the humanitarian disaster that is a toilet at a music festival, best plan ahead. Do not shit for a week prior to the festival, and the second you arrive at the grounds seek out the yet-to-be soiled portaloos and let rip. You will be evacuating such a large quantity of poo that your won't need to go again over the course of the weekend. Problem solved.

2. Lather yourself in disinfectant.

Purchase an industrial-sized vat of Dettol and mix it with a tub of vaseline. Then, coat your entire body in the thick and sanitarily sound mixture to become Portaloo-proof. With such a large quantity of disinfectant on your body, you could swim in poo for all the difference it would make.

3. Become a world squatting champion.

While most people hit the gym and squat to achieve a lovely bottom, there are more practical benefits from this exercise. If you can get your glutes, quads and calves in the best shape of their lives after months of exhausting exercise, you will have the required power to squat over a plop-infested potty for upwards of four hours, thereby avoiding all the obvious downsides to sitting.

4. Embrace the disgrace.

Fuck it, everybody poos, right? We all do it, and you'll be forgiven by your friends if you emerge from the Portaloo looking like a freshly constructed choc ice.

How to justify taking coke at Electric Picnic if you're a clean-living vegan pacifist*

It can be tough to limit the reputational damage if you're a clean-living vegan pacifist who went to town on some cocaine like you were Al Pacino in the climactic scenes of *Scarface*. Can a vegan pacifist have their cocaine cake and sniff it too? WWN is on hand to help you justify your casual drug use while simultaneously not jeopardising your well-crafted image as a quinoa- and Dalai Llama-loving so-and-so.

It's just a bit of coke, like.

Exactly. You won't touch sugar because it gave your mother's cat cancer, but coke is coke is coke. You know what you're getting with cocaine while you can't be sure what those ethically compromised sugar conglomerates are putting in sugar.

Everybody's doing it.

Exactly. This reasoning worked for you when you first did cocaine, so why shift gears and bother to look for a new excuse.

It's just a one-off.

Double exactly. This bi-weekly consumption of drugs is just a one-off, and come on, this is Electric Picnic we're talking about – you can't enjoy some of the best musical acts in the world without drugs. That's madness.

I just want a fucking burger, but that would be a betrayal of my values.

Exactly. Burger = bad. Cocaine = nowhere near as bad. Jesus, you're so convincing now, you almost believe your own bullshit.

*Note, these excuses can be used for weddings, christenings and trips to the toilet.

ELECTRIC PICNIC

BREAKING NEWS

Local man electrocuted after misunderstanding Electric Picnic

Tragedy has struck one Waterford family after a man failed to recover from injuries sustained during an ill-informed 'Electric Picnic' in his backyard.

Dungarvan native Sean O'Lennon was rushed to hospital after going into full cardiac arrest after coming into contact with a homemade contraption constructed from a picnic blanket and a car battery.

It is believed O'Lennon, known locally as a bit of a dunce, connected the electrical current to the gingham cloth after trying to recreate what he believed the 'Electric Picnic' experience to be.

'He was never the sharpest tool in the box,' admitted Cian O'Lennon, brother of the deceased.

'We asked him if he was going to Electric Picnic, and he started giving out about the price of tickets. He said he'd just have his own Electric Picnic in the backyard of his house. He showed me a schematic of the cables going to the flask of tea and the sandwiches, and I pleaded with him not to do it.

'I said, no Sean, don't do this. This is a stupid fucking idea. This is not what Electric Picnic is. But he didn't listen because he was a fucking moron.'

Mr O'Lennon's body and soul will be laid to rest later this week.

WWN guide to never leaving the Electric Picnic campsite

Do you enjoy going to music festivals purely to get absolutely off your chomp? We don't blame you; despite what others may tell you, music and arts festivals are an unmitigated hell of noise and overpriced food and drink. In fact, the best thing to do at a festival is to stay in the campsite and drink your face off while eating ham sandwiches. But how do you excuse yourself from your group for long enough to do so? Easy.

Pretend you left something back at the tent.

While your pals are pretending to like whatever awful band are banging away on the Mud & Fire stage or whatever, just excuse yourself and say you have to go back to the tent and get your wallet or something. Nobody is going to make the five-mile trek with you, and nobody is going to miss you until way later in the day. You can say 'oh, I couldn't find you', but really you've been necking tins for hours.

Fake your own death.

Tricky, but if you pretend to fall off the roof of a tent or something, your pals might be sufficiently convinced that you've passed away, allowing you to avoid being dragged from one 'awesome' poetry slam to another for half the weekend.

Clone yourself.

Send some cheek cells to China with a twenty quid note, and soon you'll have your very own stem-cell abomination, who exists only to wander around hip-deep in muck with your insufferable hippy mates, while you and three lads from Westmeath get destroyed on cans of Dutch Gold.

Eat your ticket.

'Oh no, I accidentally ate my ticket. You go on ahead – I guess I'll just stay here.' Sorted.

ELECTRIC PICNIC

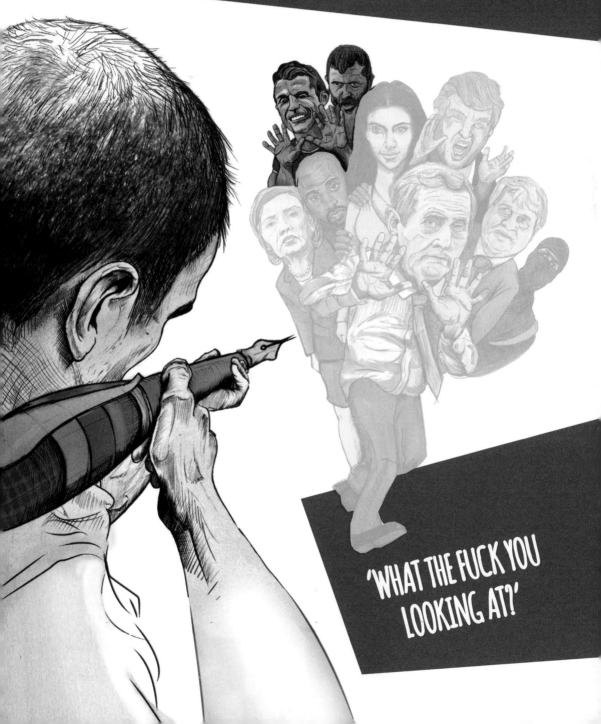

'Paul O'Connell made me feel like it was okay to be ginger'

Self-confessed ginger Killian Dermody speaks of Paul O'Connell's legacy to the ginger people of Ireland after the rugby legend's announcement that he is to retire.

I was, for much of my life, a ginger hater, which was made all the more complicated by being a raging ginger myself. I couldn't help it.

Cutting-edge medical technology couldn't catch up quick enough. They had developed a liquid you could buy and apply to your hair, but even today as ginger-hating Ireland stocks these medicines on their shelves, they're only good for a few weeks. The ginger gene is too strong, it fights back and turns whatever blonde, brown or black hair formula had been used to keep your secret back into vibrant red, strawberry blonde ... whatever way you spin it, it's ginger.

Then, fate intervened. As a teenager, during my most impressionable years, a great hulking behemoth emerged on the horizon. His name: Paul Aloysius Ferdinand O'Connell.

To others his fiery red mane said nothing, but to me it had grown some sort of mouth. Bizarre I know, but for me, a ginger child growing up in an Ireland that refused to treasure its gingers, I needed every Paul O'Connell hair utterance I could get. Each time he appeared on TV playing rugby I was transfixed.

His hair spoke in much the same way he spoke, and it said: 'Killian, you know, being ginger is actually all right, like.' I ate up every word while ignoring the more troubling fact that an Irish rugby player's hair was communicating with me.

As he excelled as a player and leader in the great Munster sides that grabbed success by the ginger pubes, I myself became emboldened. I ventured out of my house more regularly, and occasionally stopped covering up my hair with the usual eight hats. Slowly but surely, I accepted my gingerness and embraced it – until tragedy struck.

Paul shaved his head. Paul shaved his fucking head.

He had abandoned his gingerness, and as a result abandoned me. Whose fiery locks would I talk to now? I was so incensed I began cutting off locks of my hair and over weeks I put together a ginger wig and sent it in the post to Paul with the message, 'Wear me you ginger denier!', but he did not.

I was back hitting the peroxide blonde bottles pretty hard. Fifteen more trips to the doctor resulted in fifteen more 'there's no cure' diagnoses, and the inept GP was more interested in talking about the conversations I was having with other people's hair. During these dark times, one small but important detail puzzled me: Paul O'Connell was still rugbying the shite out of everyone, ginger mane or not. Irish rugby success was his. A shaven-headed hero.

Then, at last, it finally dawned on me. Paul's gingerness wasn't just in his ginger locks, it was in *him* the whole time. And so, it must be in me, too. It's in my pale skin, my freckles, even in my forest of ginger bumfluff. Cut me and I bleed ginger. Cut me and I proudly bleed ginger. Without Paul, these feelings would never have been possible.

You know, I met him once ... well, I saw him from across the road, at least I think it was him – my eyesight isn't the best. But we did lock eyes, I'm sure of that, and the look said it all. With only his eyes he said, 'You're a ginger. I'm a ginger too.'

Thank you, Paul, thank you.

CONOR McGREGOR

AGE: 27

NICKNAMES: Notorious, The Very Good Fighter Man, Conor Mouthgregor.

JOB: taking names, busting skulls.

SPECIAL TALENT: first-ever man to successfully learn to punch with his foot, and kick with his fist.

MOST MEMORABLE QUOTE: 'I am a sponge, I gather up the watery knowledge of fighting, absorbing it all. Then I allow myself to be rubbed and squeezed onto the body of my opponent, soaking them in obliteration, in the shower that is life.'

CROWNING GLORY: inventing mixed martial arts.

RESPONSIBLE FOR: eejits walking around town growing beards and wearing three-piece suits they bought in Penneys.

POTENTIAL: would be voted in as Taoiseach tomorrow if he ran.

AMBITIONS: getting paid the big bucks, being the first man to take part in a UFC bout on the moon.

Financial pearls of wisdom from Economics Correspondent Freddy Nobbs

People playing the lotto often chose rubbish numbers like 1, 13, 27 and 30. Stick to picking the good numbers, preferably the ones that end up winning the jackpot. Basic financial sense.

ROY KEANE

AGE: what sort of question is that?

OCCUPATION: ball of rage/decent stand-up comedian if he gave it a shot.

CURRENT MOOD: what the fuck you looking at?

KNOWN FOR: growing the most intense beard ever recorded in the annals of human history after getting angry one evening when he stubbed his toe on his coffee table.

PASSIONS: football, cuddling.

Maria Sharapova tests positive for bullshit excuses

In yet another blow to her sporting legacy, tennis star Maria Sharapova has tested positive for bullshit excuses and may face a further ban from the sport as a result.

Sharapova had tested positive for a substance, meldonium, which was only added to the banned substance list in January of this year, a medicine she claims she had been taking for ten years.

However, when international tennis authorities, journalists and members of the general public reviewed footage of Sharapova's press conference dealing with the positive test results, they found trace elements of 'bullshit,' a verbal substance known to be harmful to a sport star's reputation.

'It is sad that someone with so much talent would allow themselves to make such an error. Then at the press conference, I didn't notice it at first, but on replays it's very obvious she is through the roof for elements of terrible excuses,' a member of the International Tennis Federation told WWN.

Sharapova claimed in her press conference that she had been taking meldonium for ten years for a number of health problems, despite the fact that a course of the drug is normally only supposed to continue for a maximum of six weeks according to its manufacturer.

These claims, along with doubt over whether or not she ever applied for an exemption from taking the substance, sparked fears she would test positive for terrible excuses.

'You don't like to see it in an athlete as talented as Maria, but I'm not surprised the tests for excuses came back positive. The press conference was very staged-managed, conceited even. An attempt to keep endorsements perhaps?' offered sports journalist Don Smith.

Sharapova's impending ban is set to cost her millions in off-the-court endorsement deals, but her prize money on the court will not be affected as Serena Williams is planning on winning pretty much everything again this year.

EXCLUSIVE

Archaeologists confirm Mayo built on cursed Indian burial ground

As the majority of Mayo's population made the journey home from Croke Park last month, they could have been forgiven for thinking their county was cursed, and according to a recent archaeological dig it actually is.

'Playing a Dublin team who didn't turn up in the first match only to concede two own goals – it got me thinking,' TCD history professor and archaeologist Davin Hendricks explained to WWN.

'I just brought along my gear to Castlebar and had a root around and wasn't the least bit surprised to find an ancient Indian burial ground. Any county worth its salt knows that if you want to win the All-Ireland you can't go setting up your county on an ancient Indian burial ground. It's a recipe for disaster and a lengthy curse,' shared Hendricks.

'That probably explains Enda Kenny too,' Hendricks added.

With Dublin the victors in this year's All-Ireland, Mayo's wait for another taste of Sam glory continues. However, with these revelations coming to light, there is a question mark over Mayo's involvement in senior football going forward.

'Ah, we might as well pack it the fuck in. Fecking Indians – what gobshite of a councillor gave planning permission to build Mayo out here anyway? I was fooled into thinking we had a chance,' irate Westport local Seamus Borran explained to WWN.

The Mayo county board is expected to announce its withdrawal from football later this week and will not be swayed by the news that thirty counties are set to merge into one mega-county in a bid to beat Dublin next year.

Russia confirms Putin will represent nation in every Olympic sport

As the status of Russian athletes competing at the Rio Olympics changes with each passing hour, Russian leader Vladimir Putin has become so irate that he has insisted he will compete in every event and crush all opponents before him, thus defeating the politically motivated attacks against Russian athletes.

Boarding a plane for Rio this morning, Putin began lathering himself in baby oil in anticipation of taking gold in the wrestling event.

'President Putin does not care for the rules in each specific event: he will compete topless and oiled up in all of them,' a spokesperson for the Russian Olympic team explained.

While the Russian Olympic Committee (ROC) has yet to confirm how exactly Putin will compete in the female events, they have revealed that he is adept at all of the sports.

'Golf, Putin is best. 100 metres, Putin is best. Clay-pigeon shooting, Putin is best. Bear wrestling, Putin is best,' Alexi Komadov, spokesperson for the ROC confirmed, without clarifying whether or not Putin believed bear wrestling to be an Olympic event.

The Russia government also confirmed that their leader would not take any measure to guard himself against mosquitos and the Zika virus as 'the mosquitos know better than to make threats against Vladimir Putin'.

Drug-testing agencies have expressed concern at Putin's inclusion in the games, citing the only previous drugs test carried out on the politician, which revealed that his blood was 92.6 per cent testosterone.

VLADIMIR PUTIN

AGE: 64

HEIGHT: a constant source of amusement to the world.

KNOWN FOR: being President of Russia, annexing Crimea, brutally murdering his father six seconds after leaving his mother's womb.

IN THE NEWS FOR: coming to terms with the devastating loss of life suffered in the Sinai plane crash, drinking a 240-year-old bottle of Crimean wine while in a masturbation circle with Silvio Berlusconi, strangling the Loch Ness monster to death while on holiday in Scotland.

DIPLOMATIC STYLE: judo chop to the heart, loudly chewing food while holding eye contact with an adversary, throwing you over his shoulder and running away with you if you're a woman.

STRENGTHS: honestly doesn't seem to give a fuck.

WEAKNESSES: has a well-documented Freudian relationship with Mother Russia.

HOBBIES: being topless as much as possible.

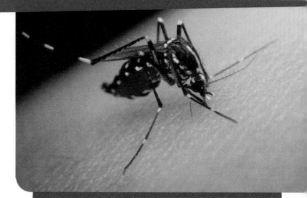

Scandal as dolphins come forward claiming to be Michael Phelps' biological parents

'We're sick of the lies. At some point you have to say "enough is enough" and stand up and be counted.'

Splashing in two paddling pools on the stage of Ellen DeGeneres's talk show, an emotional Barbara and Martin Phelps admitted they had remained silent for too long.

Squeaking to the popular daytime host, the dolphins, residents of just off the Californian coast, were quickly moved to tears.

'You probably can't tell as we're in water, but we're in floods of tears – Michael is our only son,' Martin explained.

Michael had washed ashore during a particularly violent storm in 1988 and his parents were unable to retrieve him. Having searched for years they saw him on TV at the Beijing Olympics in 2008.

'I turned to Martin and said, 'That's our boy," didn't I, Martin? He had his father's breaststroke technique – it was uncanny,' Barbara cackled in an annoyingly high register.

Attempts to reunite with their talented son were blocked by US swimming officials.

'They explained that he would be stripped of his medals, on account of him being revealed as being 100 per cent dolphin, and we didn't want to compromise his success. But after he won twenty-two golds we said fuck it, this is getting ridiculous,' Martin added, speaking of his son's obvious advantage in the pool over his human rivals.

Michael, for his part, has always denied being a dolphin, but Olympic officials are now looking into the claims. Concluding the interview, Barbara and Martin admitted they believed reconciliation with their son would not be possible.

'He has a very different life to us now – lucrative contracts and a child of his own. All we do is swim around the ocean all day,' Barbara said, sobbing from her blowhole.

'I've been waiting for this day for fucking months,' says Zika mosquito as golf begins

'Frankly there has been a lot of shite talked over the last few weeks and months and I'm just looking to put that behind me now that the golf is starting. I'm ready to compete.'

These are the words of Buzz the mosquito, a Rio-based parasite looking to make his mark on the 2016 games. You can appreciate where Buzz is coming from; he's been slandered, defamed and his name has been dragged through the mud but now the talking is over.

'You just want to get out there and do what you do best as a virus-carrying mosquito,' he added, while repeatedly charging a net in one of the bedrooms at the Olympic village.

There have been injunctions issued against leading golfers, with McIlroy, Spieth and Day among their number. A campaign to restore Buzz's good name is under way, but now all that is left to do is produce the goods.

'Oh, trust me, my plan is to get out and really put myself about. The time for talking is done, the time for fucking shit-up has begun,' a determined Buzz added, admitting the golf represented his best chance of success at the games.

'The indoor events don't agree with me. I'm best operating out in the open and, in fairness, the golf course is immaculate. Who wouldn't want to perform in those conditions?'

Buzz can be seen at the golfing event in Rio today.

Scumbag Olympics confirmed for Dublin city centre next week

Dublin City has received a huge boost with the news that is has been chosen as the host city for this year's Scumbag Olympics, a sister competition to the Summer Olympics, which took place in Rio in August.

The Scumbag Olympics will last three weeks and take in a variety of events which will bring in €100 million to the local economy. However, considering the nature of the events, the games could also see the local economy robbed of over €300 million.

Events range from the fastest pickpocket, the quickest unlocking of a stolen iPhone, the 100-yard dash away from Gardaí, kicking a stranger's head in and countless others which should horrify and enthral the public in equal measure.

Despite the international flavour of the upcoming games, Team Ireland's coach is confident of some medal success.

'There's lads coming over from Nigeria, America, Australia, Romania, China and so on, but we feel we've put in the years of practice necessary to win,' Decco 'The Nutter' Kelly explained to WWN.

Any medal wins for Ireland would be a huge boost to scumbagism in the country, with eyes firmly fixed on Sarah and Alan O'Connor, who remain the hot favourites in the loudest public shouting-match event.

'This proves our scumbags can compete at the highest international level, and we as a nation should be proud of that,' Taoiseach Enda Kenny stated after receiving confirmation of the event.

Waterford young fella qualifies for Olympic shape-throwing finals

Waterford young fella Danny Phelan made history today in Brazil when he became the first ever shape-thrower from Ireland to qualify for the finals in Rio.

The 22-year-old from Larchville will compete for his country against twenty-four other competitors from around the world this week.

Phelan smashed his previous record by throwing over twenty different shapes while walking the 1,000-metre course this morning, smashing everyone in his heat.

Throwing shapes only became recognised as an Olympic sport last year and has since become hugely popular among young 'townies' across the country.

'I started throwing shapes when I was 13 and it kind of took off from

there,' said Phelan, 'I suppose it was a defence thing in a way, to make meself look bigger and that.'

Danny's manager and father, Tom Phelan, said his son was one of the biggest shapers he has seen in Ireland in a long time and expects a gold from him this year.

'I tell ya one thing, bai, if he doesn't win something I'll show him fucking shapes,' he half-joked with a serious face.

The shape-throwing event spans over 1000 metres, with nine competitors trying to throw the highest number of shapes in the quickest time possible. Competitors will be marked on arm sway, outward feet position, chest pump and intimidating head posture. At least one 'do-you-want-your-go' shape must be thrown during each 1000-metre dash. The winner of the shape-throwing event will receive a gold chain instead of a gold medal.

'I will pay off Ireland's remaining debt for Christmas' — Conor McGregor

UFC Featherweight Champion Conor McGregor has confirmed today that he will pay off Ireland's debt for Christmas, in one of his most generous gestures to date.

The Crumlin-born mixed-martial-arts expert said it would be an honour for him to clear the country's balance from the IMF books, stating it was the least he could do.

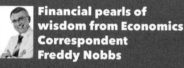

'Magic Mac is back in town, baby, and when Magic Mac spends, he spends good,' McGregor told a congregation of fans on Grafton Street this afternoon while shopping with friends. 'We should look into getting a roof for this city, some gold-plated railings around the Liffey, a nice diamond on the end of the Spire.'

Currently Ireland owes €204.4 billion in state debt, a figure the Irish fighter scoffed at.

'Please, I'll make that in one round in Croke Park,' he taunted, pretending that he was writing a cheque. 'When the IMF gets a taste of this left hand, it's all over … BOOM, debts out for the count baby, yeah!'

On hearing the news, Taoiseach Enda Kenny thanked Mr McGregor for his kind donation, stating the UFC star is a testament to the bravery and courage of the Irish people.

WORLD SPORT

A successful Olympic Games came to a stunning conclusion last night in the Maracana Stadium as teams gathered to enjoy the closing ceremony in Rio.

While impressive firework displays are now part and parcel of such ceremonies, the Rio games organisers had a surprise in store for international audiences watching from around the world.

A blinding spotlight, guiding people's attention skyward,

Rio closing ceremony finishes with stunning suspension of Pat Hickey in a cage over stadium

beamed towards the roof of the stadium where a tired-looking Pat Hickey was lowered from the rooftop in a cage, in a tribute to the Brazilian authorities' zero tolerance policy on wrongdoing during the three weeks the Olympics were being held in Rio.

'A delight, a vista of stunning imagination, a ceremony very much cast from a mould befitting modern Olympic times,' mused the *New York Times* review of the closing ceremony, illustrating just what a triumph these games had been in many respects.

Hickey for his part looked a reluctant participant in the carnival-themed celebration below his reinforced-steel cage, with many people on Twitter criticising him for not dancing. His decision not to wear a dressing gown also drew considerable ire.

The Olympics had been dogged by accusations that clean athletes were competing fairly to win medals and had been surrounded by brazen positivity. However, the closing ceremony acknowledged that this wasn't the dominant theme of the 2016 games.

EURO 2016 SOUVENIR SPECIAL

Ireland's most iconic Euro moments

Ireland's rich and varied history at the Euros contains a vast array of unforgettable moments that other nations will be hard pushed to surpass. WWN looks back with fondness at the thrilling adventures that our boys in green have provided us with over the years:

Euro 1960: we weren't there. Zero craic.

Euro 1964: see above.

Euro 1968: you get the picture.

Euro 1972: we were fairly close to getting to this one.

Euro 1976: ah, we weren't missing much, to be honest.

Euro 1980: we were busy with other things – sheds needed to be cleared out, things brought down from the attic.

Euro 1984: minus craic.

Euro 1988: Ray Houghton's goal against England secured Ireland a famous piss-up some of us still haven't recovered from.

Euro 1992: Denmark won, that was a bit mad. But, yeah, we sat this one out.

Euro 1996: got a bit of mileage out of how funny it was watching England think they'd actually win it.

Euro 2000: we aren't very good at this going to the Euros lark.

Euro 2004: Thomas Murphy from Lismore was seen on one of the big screens: proud day for the whole country. Still not sure what he was doing at the Euros though.

Euro 2008: Nope. Nothing. But on the plus side John Delaney got a pay rise of €78 million.

Euro 2012: Giovanni Trapattoni's men gave us no other option than to drown our sorrows.

Euro 2016: Robbie Brady's header gave Ireland its greatest excuse to call in sick to work since Wes Hoolahan's goal against Sweden several days earlier.

 The Year in Stats

60% of normally polite people turn into complete psychopaths for the duration of five-a-side football matches.

Housewives advised to bury savings after Ireland qualify for Euro 2016

In a special announcement from the Central Bank Commission, housewives across the country are being advised to bury their savings in a discreet location after Ireland qualified for the 2016 UEFA European Championship last night.

The announcement came almost immediately after the Republic of Ireland beat Bosnia 2-0 at the Aviva Stadium, securing their place in the finals with a 3-1 win on aggregate.

Housewives across the country got up extra early today to make the trip to banks, building societies and credit unions, emptying their joint accounts and withdrawing their savings.

Many of these women took the cash, some of it amounting to thousands, and hid it throughout the house for safekeeping. In some instances, the cash was sealed in a waterproof container and buried in the backyard, where husbands and partners would not be able to find it and blow it all on a trip to Paris to see Ireland eke out a series of scoreless draws.

'You can fit nearly ten thousand euros in a Colman's mustard jar,' read the commission's statement. 'This can then be wrapped in clingfilm, then put into a jam jar, and silicone mastic pumped in around it. This should allow you to keep your cash safe until Euro 2016 is over. Most banks and building societies have been contacted, and a special system is in place where your interest rates and savings schemes will hold until you re-lodge the cash in August.'

Meanwhile, the Financial Regulator has also put a series of blocks in place to prevent people taking out loans for 'renovations' over the next nine months.

England fans wasting no time this year

Anticipating a first-round exit from the Euro 2016 competition, England fans have taken it upon themselves to get into as many riots and scraps as they can while their campaign for glory lasts.

Tear gas was used by riot police in Marseille yesterday as England fans kicked off with French authorities before a ball had even been kicked in the tournament.

Two fans were arrested in the scuffles, putting the England team at a distinct disadvantage before their first game against Russia today at 8 p.m.

'We really needed them two lads in the stands, cheering us on,' said one source close to the England squad.

'That leaves us with two less voices, with the possibility that more will be arrested after cops check CCTV. We've got a pretty shit line-up this year, and we could do with every pair of lungs we can get. If anyone out there wants to start some shit with French cops, then by all means do. But at least wait until we've got to the end of the group stages.'

Republic of Ireland fans have also reached France and are continuing to be the absolute best fans of anyone anywhere in the world, although French authorities have asked that they keep the craic to a minimum as they're just too amazing sometimes.

EURO 2016 SOUVENIR SPECIAL

Irish fans sell 'The Fields of Athenry' to Northern Ireland for €75 million

With news emerging that the Northern Ireland football team may not be able to use 'God Save the Queen' as their national anthem at the upcoming Euro 2016 finals, Irish supporters have come forward and offered to sell the rights to 'The Fields Of Athenry' to their northern neighbours for a cool €75 million.

The use of 'God Save the Queen' is in jeopardy following the proposal of a new bill by MPs in the House of Commons, which states that as the song is the national anthem of the United Kingdom as a whole, it should not be used as the national anthem for individual members of the UK.

The use of the anthem had been in debate for some years, with many Northern Irish athletes opting for 'Danny Boy' to be played as they received their medals at last year's Commonwealth Games.

With the debate still raging in Stormont, representatives for supporters of the Republic of Ireland have put forth an offer to sell one of their most beloved terrace tunes, 'The Fields Of Athenry.'

'We've got songs to spare, so the Nordies can have this one if they're willing to pay for it,' said Sean Logan, spokesperson for The Best Fans in the World™.

'€75 million is a fair price to ask for one of the most anthemic songs in the history of the sport. As a bonus, the song will also be confiscated from Glasgow Celtic, and Northern Ireland can let Rangers sing it as well if they like.'

Neither Scotland nor Wales are using 'God Save the Queen' and England seems likely to follow suit. If a deal is not found soon then Northern Ireland may find itself without an anthem to stand to during Euro 2016 before they get knocked out at the group stages.

Paris crisp touts selling packets of Tayto for €30 each

Irish fans travelling to the European Championships in France are being warned to avoid purchasing Tayto crisps from street touts, as many packets have been reported to be counterfeit.

So far over two hundred complaints have been made over the illegal touts, many of whom are selling single packets for as much as €30.

'I got four packets for €100, but when I opened them they didn't taste the same. Robbed we were,' one victim told WWN, who somehow managed to forget to pack his suitcase with the Irish-made potato crisp, like a big eejit.

'I've since asked for an emergency supply to be sent over, and that should be here before the Ireland game,' he added. He has even got in touch with Mr Tayto and asked him to help another spud out.

Irish fans who have yet to travel to France are being urged to stock up on Tayto before leaving to avoid disappointment.

EURO 2016 SOUVENIR SPECIAL

Iceland more or less forgiven for that whole ash-cloud craic

The world has decided to forgive Iceland for the 2010 eruptions of the volcano Eyjafjallajökull following the plucky *Mighty Ducks*-style performance of their national football team at the Euro 2016 tournament in France.

The eruption of the volcano in 2010 caused widespread travel chaos across Europe, as air traffic controllers were forced to ground airplanes for days on end due to the high level of ash in the air.

The ensuing hassle of flight cancellations and holiday rescheduling soured both Iceland and everything Icelandic for many people for years, although all seems to have been forgiven after they dumped England out of the Euros with an unbelievable 2-1 win during the last-sixteen stage of the tournament.

'I was stuck in Malta for two weeks with no hotel and no money because of that fucking ash cloud,' said one former Iceland hater. 'But then you see them stick it to the English, and follow it up with a sweet Viking haka type of a thing … well, you just have to say all is forgiven, don't you?'

The Iceland football team have been assured that should they manage to beat France in their quarter-final fixture this weekend, the world may actually forgive them for Björk as well.

Irish fans reaching critical levels of soundness

Fears are growing that Irish fans in France for the Euro 2016 football championship may be about to hit peak soundness, with experts warning that they have no idea what will happen when the green army run out of ways to endear themselves to the world.

Fans from all over Ireland descended on France last week ahead of the Republic of Ireland's campaign, and immediately set about being as sound as they possibly could, through a series of hilarious chants, hilarious slogans on flags, and hilarious acts of charity and goodwill.

Although the world currently loves the Irish, there is growing dread about what might happen if the boys in green do something so sound that it can't be topped.

'We're looking at the complete collapse of the soundness bubble,' said one soundness analyst, speaking exclusively to WWN.

'And we're looking at it soon. There's only so much the Irish fans can do before their soundness becomes irritating. And the day is coming soon. Last week, they changed a flat tyre for an old couple. Today, they helped a lady deliver a baby in the back of a Clio. And there's word coming in that Irish fans are flooding French hospitals to donate a kidney to whoever needs one … this is unsustainable.'

Should the soundness bubble pop, there are fears that Irish fans may never be able to get the validation that they're 'very good' that they need to continue supporting the Irish soccer team.

EURO 2016 SOUVENIR SPECIAL

'Ireland is saving itself for the World Cup anyway,' confirms O'Neill

Ireland manager Martin O'Neill confirmed what many Irish fans suspected: that the boys in green only lost to France yesterday in order to better prepare for winning the World Cup in two years' time.

O'Neill confessed to being incredibly proud of his players, but confirmed they were all in agreement before kick-off that they would bow out in order to prepare for winning the World Cup in Russia, which at this point is a mere formality.

'There's just so much planning involved, as I'm sure you can imagine. We've had to put in a special order at breweries for the parade we'll have in Dublin with the trophy. So we thought it best to get cracking on those small details early,' O'Neill explained.

The manager confirmed that Robbie Brady's penalty in the opening minutes was not planned and was a result of the players 'getting a bit excited' but the game plan, which will ultimately see Ireland beat England in the final 1916-0, was kicked back into gear resulting in a 2-1 loss.

'We were conscious of the fact that if we took the game to extra time, many of the fans in the stadium might miss the train or the bus they had planned on getting. It would have been very selfish of us to disrupt anyone's plans,' O'Neill confirmed.

'And you have to remember, France were in front of their home fans. It would have been nothing short of rude if we had beat them. We'll save it for when we win the World Cup in Moscow,' the former Sunderland boss concluded.

Top 7 laughs in Ireland in 2016

7. A ha
6. Mwaaaah ha ha ha
5. Huh huh huh
4. Hahahahaha
3. Bah ha
2. Tee hee
1. Bwaaaaaaah haha haha

Fitness Tips from Expert Fiachra Burley

Kegels, when done right, can tighten things down there to the point where women no longer need to ask men to open jars of food for them.

Fitness Tips from Expert Fiachra Burley

It is absolutely pointless working out in the gym if it's empty. It's important to have an audience.

Head Ray Houghton used to score against England put on public display

Euro fever gripped Ireland again this year as Martin O'Neill's men secured a famous victory against Italy and pushed France close in a 2-1 defeat.

These treasured new memories – Wes Hoolahan's goal against Sweden and Robbie Brady's header against Italy among them – have prompted a renewed interest in one of the biggest victories in Ireland's footballing history: our historic 1-0 defeat of England in Euro '88.

Over the years, memorabilia relating to Ireland's exploits in Italia '90 and USA '94 have sold for thousands at auction, with the gloves Packie Bonner used to save the penalty taken by Romania's Daniel Timofte fetching €19 million in 2002.

However, possibly the most sought-after piece of Irish football memorabilia comes in the form of Ray Houghton's head, which was used to guide the ball past England's Peter Shilton at Euro '88. Houghton had been famously unwilling to part with his head, but after hearing how much a private collector was willing to pay for it, the head is now set to be put on display by the buyer in the National Gallery.

'I've grown quite fond of my head, and it's been responsible for a lot of great memories I've had in a green jersey, but I think it's only right I sell it on to someone who wants to put it on public display so as many people get to relive that much cherished memory,' Houghton explained to WWN, shortly before parting ways with his head.

EURO 2016 SOUVENIR SPECIAL

Where are they now? Ireland's Euro 2016 fans

No set of fans gave a better account of themselves and left a more lasting impression at Euro 2016 than the green army. Thousands of Irish people singing in the streets, charming the French people and the world's media – there has scarcely been a more enduring sight to come out of a sporting tournament than our dedicated fans, but where have they all gone now? WWN tracked a number of them down.

Ciaran Duffy (21): video of him performing open heart surgery on fourteen people on top of the Eiffel Tower after a rare outbreak of contagious heart attacks – 556,000 views on YouTube.

'NASA gave me a call once I got home,' Duffy told WWN from his new home in Cape Cod. 'They are seriously worried about offending any alien life we may encounter in the future, so I've been drafted in to head up a new unit and given the title of Chief Banter Engineer. I loved the Euros, but I think I love the new job even more.'

Davey Cummins (29): video of Davey curing cancer by starting a chant of 'cure cancer for the boys in green' went viral on 345 Irish websites that offer unique, one-of-a-kind content to all their readers – 700,000 views.

'Curing cancer was a great bit of banter, but then I was getting a lot of criticism online for not stopping HIV, Ebola and Zika as well.

Thought that was overly harsh,' Cummins explains from his office in New York. 'But now in my new role as head of the UN, I will give that stuff my best shot too.'

Sean Ginnerty (24): 134 separate videos of Sean shouting 'Olé, Olé, Olé' went viral on Joe.ie – 4.5 million views.

'When I came home, I thought I couldn't replicate the craic that was over there, but then one of my mates suggested we get pissed at home in Mullingar and sing 'Olé Olé Olé' there, and it's almost as good.'

Alan Gough (33): video of Alan rescuing a breakfast roll from a burning building in Lyon went viral – 123 million views.

'It's going well, 'twas a bit of a comedown from the excitement after the Euros naturally, but this new cushy government job is the business,' Alan shared. The 33-year-old is part of a group of more than thirty thousand Irish men that the government has sent abroad on a holiday to spread craic globally while conveniently reducing the number of unemployed on the register.

Stevie Hughes (19): a video of Stevie in the Louvre in Paris went viral after he tucked the Mona Lisa under his shirt and walked out the emergency exit.

'Ah you just don't get the same level of banter back home,' Stevie explained from his prison cell in France. 'And yeah, I'm doing ten years in prison here, but you can't beat the craic. It was class.'

The Year in Stats

There has been a 17% increase in the use of the word 'geebag' as the swear word's popular resurgence continues.

EURO 2016 SOUVENIR SPECIAL